SUCCESS

ACCELERATION

SUCCESS

ACCELERATION

TONY JEARY

RIVER
OAK
PUBLISHING

Tulsa, Oklahoma

06 05 04 03   10 09 08 07 06 05 04 03 02

Success Acceleration
Hardback edition ISBN 1-58919-978-2
Paperback edition ISBN 1-58919-992-8
Copyright © 2002 by Tony Jeary

Published by RiverOak Publishing
P.O. Box 700143
Tulsa, Oklahoma 74170-0143

DEDICATION

To my two beautiful daughters, Brooke and Paige, with the hope and prayer that one day they will both utilize these principles in their own lives to accelerate their personal success.

ACKNOWLEDGMENTS

I would like to acknowledge and thank a few special people who contributed much to the development and publication of this work: First, my long-term friend, Jim Norman, who spent many hours helping me fine-tune and organize this message. My former executive assistant, Nonie Jobe, who spent countless hours helping me rework the manuscript to get it ready to submit for publication. My literary agent, Bruce Barbour, for helping me place this work with the right publisher. My friend and publisher, Mark Gilroy, for his continued support and belief in the importance of accelerating success. And finally, Rick Davis and Mark Magnacca, my two good friends and colleagues who offered their support and helped me formulate the concepts for this work.

TABLE OF CONTENTS

FOREWORD

BY BRIAN TRACY

This is the greatest time in all of human history to be alive. There have never been more opportunities and possibilities for the average person to achieve great success in personal and financial life than exist today. Our job is to take full advantage of this wonderful environment and become everything we are capable of becoming. This wonderful book by Tony Jeary, *Success Acceleration*, will give you a series of foundational principles, strategies, and essential tactics that you can use to increase the speed at which you move toward your goals.

Whether you are aware of it or not, you have within you, right now, talents and abilities that you have never fully realized. You have greater intelligence and creativity than you have yet utilized. You have a greater capacity for happiness and joy than you have ever imagined. Within these pages you will learn how to get the very most out of yourself, both as an individual and in your relationships with others. You will learn how to set better goals, make better plans, and develop better strategies for achieving those goals—on schedule. When you follow the simple, practical, proven principles that Tony teaches you in this book, you will actually step on the accelerator of your own potential. You will move faster toward the achievement of the things you really want in life than perhaps you ever believed possible. You will learn how to release your brakes and step on the gas.

Tony Jeary is one of the most insightful and intelligent writers, thinkers, speakers, and presenters in America today. He has assembled a blueprint that you can follow to create a wonderful life for yourself and the people you care about the most. Get ready for an exciting ride!

M ost people have an innate desire to be successful in every area of
their lives—personal, family, and business. Thousands of books
and articles have been written on the subject. Resources abound on how
to be a successful investor, a successful writer, a successful parent, a
successful spouse—a successful anything. With so much material available, it is interesting to consider why success still eludes so many.

Because success is so subjective and can be evaluated by so many
different standards, it is difficult to define. Some measure success in
terms of money and material possessions. Some, by degrees of power and
influence. Others, by relationships; and still others, by spiritual or
emotional criteria. God's view of success, as found in the Bible (particularly in the book of Proverbs), has to do with having a good reputation,
moral character, and the spiritual devotion to obey Him.

Whatever the yardstick, it appears that success is in short supply for
the majority of Americans. More than 50 percent of new marriages in this
country will end in divorce this year. It appears that more children are
taking drugs than at any other time in our history. Addiction and treat-
ment facilities are full. Church attendance is down, and public figures are
not trusted or respected. Only 5 percent of the workforce in this country
will earn more than $100,000 a year in the first part of the new century.

Personal debt in America is at an all-time high, while personal savings are declining. Based on these facts, success by any definition is a scarce commodity. And yet, most people say they want to be more successful.

Obviously, by the fact that you are reading this book, you want to make some changes in your life that will positively affect your level of achievement. I want to compliment you for taking that first step, and I sincerely believe reading this book will energize and inspire you to make the necessary changes to accelerate your success.

By many standards, I am considered successful. I have an extremely comfortable home and earn very nice fees for my area of expertise, working closely with some of the world's top organizations such as Ford, Wal-Mart, and New York Life. I have what I consider a very enjoyable and secure relationship with a strong and loving family. I am on intimate terms with God and value His direction, and I focus first and foremost on following His plans for success in every area of my life.

However, do these "symptoms" of success really prove that I have been successful? For almost twenty-five years I have been a serious student of success and achievement. I have read and studied incredible amounts of material written and spoken by the greatest experts on achievement in the world. Og Mandino, Napoleon Hill, Norman Vincent Peale, Zig Ziglar, Earle Nightingale, Brian Tracy, and many others have had significant influence in my development and personal success.

As I studied these successful individuals and put their principles into practice, I began to develop my own ideas and strategies about success and personal achievement. I found certain shortcuts to success and discovered that some achievement principles were more effective than others. I realized that certain foundational principles actually drive and support other success factors, and that the learning curve for acquiring and utilizing success principles could be quickened.

The premise of *Success Acceleration* is that the process of achieving success can be expedited if we are willing to change. In this book I discuss three key elements in the process of success acceleration: foundations, strategies, and tactics. If a person can truly understand why he does the things he does (establish the foundation), become aware of the things he needs to do (build the strategy), and change his actions accordingly (apply the tactics), he can quicken personal achievement. This may sound too easy, or it may sound too difficult. The truth is, it is both. The difference is found in a person's *willingness* to change. If he is not willing to change, he won't. If he is willing to change, he will. It is that simple. When a willingness to change connects with the right success principles and action steps, the inevitable result is an acceleration of personal achievement.

Section One:

FOUNDATIONS

THE BELIEF WINDOW

One of the most powerful concepts I have ever discovered has proven to be a pillar in the foundation of accelerated success. As I have applied this truth in my own life and shared it with thousands of others whom I coach and teach, it has been exciting to watch it consistently produce resounding results.

Whether we know it or not, we all conduct our lives and make decisions based on our principles. *If* those principles are accurate, they will help us make right choices. Understanding how our principles govern our decisions is one of the most dynamic concepts in quickening our success.

Simply put, our outlook on the world around us is determined by our *belief windows*. We filter life and process information through the principles we begin forming from birth. These principles create a belief window that affects everything we see, hear, and experience. We form our life "rules"

> *Understanding how our principles govern our decisions is one of the most dynamic concepts in quickening our success.*

based on these beliefs, and then we establish a behavior pattern according to our rules. Unless we are operating our lives with flawless principles, we are probably not achieving the level of success we want. Understanding this foundational concept is a big step that can catapult us toward quickening achievement.

While studying success over the years, I have worked with much diligence and discipline to get the right principles in my own belief window. Fortunately, my parents and grandparents helped me form many positive beliefs, but not all of them were completely accurate. Likewise, some outstanding teachers and other mentors influenced me greatly—but some of their perceptions and beliefs were faulty. I have devoted many years to studying and forming *right* principles, and I want to share some of them with you to help you build a solid foundation for accelerated success.

As we go through life, we are constantly making value judgments, forming opinions, interpreting events, and making decisions about the things we will and will not do. Our belief windows function as filtering devices that often allow only the information we deem important to pass through, and they can screen out information we don't *think* we need. Our choices and actions always reveal the principles in our belief windows.

> *"A lie gets halfway around the world before the truth has a chance to get its pants on."*
>
> —Sir Winston Churchill

What happens if our belief windows contain erroneous principles? Obviously, there will be significant errors in the way information is filtered; and events, ideas, and our choices will be affected. Racism, for example, is an erroneous principle surrounding a particular race of people. If we embrace that belief and take actions accordingly, it can lead us to serious consequences. Similarly, if we believe that most people are insincere and have hidden agendas, it will be difficult for us to trust others or ever form close relationships. If we have a faulty belief about something that is significant for achievement, it could keep us from taking an important step toward success—and even cause us to fail.

While teaching my clients and students over the years, I have often emphasized that the most important element of this concept is that our principles *must* be accurate if we want to accelerate success. Since everything we do is based on the principles in our belief windows, we have to constantly adjust our beliefs to point us in the right direction. There is always room for improvement if we want to quicken achievement and have more success.

Let me give you an example. I have chosen to live by the principle that people in general are competent and that a smile will go a long way toward getting people to do what I want or need. When I approach the ticket counter at the airport with a smile and say, "Hi, I was hoping you might be able to help me," the ticket agent will almost always go the extra mile to accommodate me. Instead, if I believed that people in general were incompetent, I might go up to the counter with a stern face and berate the agent and the airline. Would I get the same results? Probably not.

As we grow and mature through life, we go through the process of changing the principles in our belief windows—for better or worse. We make choices every day that determine the condition of our belief windows. When we reach the point of realizing that we have control over what goes into our belief windows, and that we can take control of our actions by performing "surgery" on the principles that reside there, we will be on the brink of accelerated success.

WHAT WE BELIEVE

Insecurities caused by false principles in your belief window produce fear—and fear paralyzes success.

Our belief windows have enormous power, because they contain all of the life principles we embrace. Our principles form the foundation of who we are. They are held at the very core of our being, and it is vital that they be true and correct.

Since who we are, what we believe, how we relate to those around us, what actions we take, and ultimately the success we achieve all stem from the principles in our belief windows, it is critical that those principles be based on truth. A popular belief today is that truth is "relative." However, real and absolute truth is based solely on the Bible. Jesus said, "I am the way and the truth and the life" (John 14:6). He also told us, "If you hold

22

adjustments for the rest of our lives! As we grow older, the adjustments in most cases will become fewer and more difficult. As we mature, we embrace the life principles that are most important to us. Even though some of these core principles may not be entirely accurate, it is difficult to change them because we believe them to be absolutely true and have operated with them for a long time.

"Each problem that I solved became a rule which served afterwards to solve other problems."

—RENE DESCARTES

We spent a lot of time as children learning things. We learned from our experiences; from our parents; and from brothers, sisters, and friends. We learned some things the hard way and were sometimes hurt in the process. Harsh lessons usually make a more vivid impression and are remembered much longer. Whatever the means or the source, we formed beliefs as we learned our lessons, and the sum of all those beliefs makes us the unique people we are. No two people will live identical lives and experience the same things, in the same order, at the same age, and get the same results. Even though our cultural experiences will be similar enough to produce many common beliefs, our individual beliefs will be like a fingerprint. Nobody will believe exactly as we do about everything, because no one else has lived our life.

THE THINGS WE BELIEVE CONTROL OUR LIVES

Our beliefs usually fall into three broad categories: (1) principles we believe to be true; (2) principles we believe to be false; and (3) principles we do not yet believe are either true or false. As we go through life and learn, we are continually forming beliefs about whether things are true or false, right or wrong, appropriate or inappropriate. The problem is that our experiences are imperfect and, consequently, we sometimes make bad decisions based on imperfect beliefs. No person is immune to this error. I suspect that even the wisest people on earth have some principles in their belief windows that are not true.

History is filled with examples of people who have believed things to be true that were not. Medical doctors used to believe that bleeding their patients would drain disease from their bodies. Today, doctors would probably lose their licenses if they employed such treatments. The point is, no matter how well intentioned we may be or how sincerely we want to be objective, it is difficult to determine true things based solely on our opinions and our own experiences.

"Education is a progressive discovery of our own ignorance."

—WILL DURANT

We have all been strongly influenced by the way we were raised and the things we saw our parents do. Young couples who become engaged and participate in pre-marital counseling will probably discover areas in the relationship that present possibilities for conflict. If they grew up in different types of families, there could be huge differences of opinion about the role each should play in the relationship. If, for example, a young woman was raised in a home where her father regularly helped her mother with the housework, she would probably expect this same behavior from her future husband. However, her fiancé would most likely emulate the behavior of his own father, who may have never lifted a finger to do housework. These areas of disagreement expose the different principles in their respective belief windows. They are the result of their unique experiences and represent their individuality; yet these same beliefs can set the stage for unmet expectations, resentment, and many disagreements.

The beginning of strife is like letting out water; so quit before the quarrel breaks out.

—PROVERBS 17:14
RSV

This is a good place to point out that communication, or the lack of it, affects our belief windows. In order to have a truly successful marriage, for example, we have to communicate (really communicate) on a regular basis; when we do, we will change some of the principles in our belief windows. In this previous example of the engaged couple, each believes his or her perspective to be true, when in fact neither of their opinions represents the whole truth. The issue here is not whether husbands should help their wives do housework. The issue is that both husband and wife believe something to be true that is not true, and it has the potential to negatively affect their relationship. Using the tool of communication, the couple can discuss the issue and reach an agreement that both can approve and accept—changing their belief windows to match.

We will discuss in a later chapter the four stages of awareness or competence. However, I want to mention here that when we are in a state of *unconscious incompetence* (not even knowing that we don't know) on any given subject, we actually believe something to be true that is not true. Let's say, for example, that we don't even know what a computer is or does. That being the case, perhaps we would believe that we have little use for a computer. The *truth* is that we would have many potential uses for a computer if we just knew what a computer does and how to use one. This knowledge would mean that our belief that we have little use for a computer simply is not true.

How many areas of unconscious incompetence do you think you might have? Unless you are perfectly educated and informed—having mastered every conceivable subject, art form, and life stage—it is probably fair to say that there are principles in your belief window that may need adjusting. More than likely, you have at least a few erroneous principles that are keeping you from having accelerated success.

CHOICES

The choices we make on a daily basis probably number in the thousands. Obviously, some are more important than others, but the total number of choices we make each day would astound us if they could all be counted. We make choices about the work we do, what we wear, what we say, where we go, and countless other things. Some of

our decisions are made subconsciously, and
others require thought and deliberation. Our
lives are consumed with options, whether
simple or complex, and every choice we
make is controlled and processed through
our belief windows.

*Every choice we
make is controlled
and processed
through our
belief windows.*

To demonstrate again how beliefs affect
our choices, let me give you an example from
my own life. My parents and grandparents
owned a very successful car detail business.
They operated their business with the belief
that it was extremely important to know at all times where they stood on
cash flow and business volume so they could project future business and
make prudent decisions. So every afternoon, without fail, they would
reconcile the cash, checks, and receipts in the drawer and make detailed
records of their business. I adopted that same belief. I subsequently
made the choice that, as a business person, I would go far beyond normal
accounting procedures and keep virtually a daily business pro forma that
would let me know at all times where I am, where I am going, and how
much it will take to get there.

The point is, I made the choice to do this based on the things I
believe; because I have made that choice, I have been able to accelerate
my success in many areas. At the early age of twenty-three, I was a self-
made millionaire—but just four short years later I found myself insol-
vent. I now realize I did not have *all* of the correct principles concerning

management and risks. I have since corrected those management and risk principles in my belief window, and for over a decade now I have again enjoyed a very successful business and personal life. With every choice we make, we process all the information we have available and make the choice based on our most dominant beliefs.

You may already be very successful. On the other hand, you may have struggled with achievement and may not be as successful as you would like. Whichever the case, it may be a good idea to look at the choices you have made and the principles governing those choices. Regardless of your current achievement level, you can always improve.

You picked up this book because you wanted to accelerate your success. The very foundation of success acceleration is the fact that some of the principles you have in your belief window are not completely accurate, and they must be changed. Change the principles in your belief window that are not true, and you will be well on your way to accelerated success.

⚐

⚐   Understanding how our principles govern our decisions is one of the most dynamic concepts in quickening our success.

⚐   Insecurities caused by false principles in your belief window produce fear—and fear paralyzes success.

⚐   Communication, or the lack of it, affects our belief windows.

⚐   When we are in a state of *unconscious incompetence*, we actually believe something to be true that is not true.

⚐   Every choice we make is controlled and processed through our belief windows.

2

A WELL-MANAGED LIFE

If you have started to seriously consider the accuracy of the principles in your belief window, you have taken the first step toward building a solid foundation for accelerated success. The second essential element in that foundation is a well-managed life. Those who lack good life-management skills will have difficulty sustaining the discipline needed to produce continued success. If you hope to be a high achiever, it is absolutely critical that you maintain discipline in your life. Consistent discipline will continually move you toward success as you set your goals, make your plans to reach them, and work to accomplish your objectives.

There are six basic elements common to all human existence, and how we combine them provides the evidence of life management. This concept is also known as the "Balance Wheel of Life," and it embraces the principle that the more balanced we are in each of the six areas, the smoother our "wheel" of life will roll.

Those who lack good life-management skills will have difficulty sustaining the discipline needed to produce continued success.

> "Only I can change
> my life. No one
> can do it for me."
>
> —CAROL BURNETT

While these categories are fairly simple, life is certainly much more complicated than this list might imply. It is the interaction and application of these six areas that can be, and usually are, very difficult. Every individual's life is a journey marked by thousands of events. If we were to analyze everything that occurs in the course of a person's life, we would find that each event falls into one or more of these six basic categories:

Spiritual

Social

Educational

Home and Family

Physical and Health

Financial

We will discuss the important role that goal setting plays in achieving accelerated success in greater depth during a later chapter. But setting personal goals within these six basic areas is the key to developing a well-managed life. The best way to get your wheel out of balance is to simply "let life happen" and not establish goals in each of these areas. Unfortunately, many people live their lives without setting goals, and the result is a that a large percentage of our society is simply drifting through life with no place to go, so to speak. Many people who hope to be successful are just waiting for their "big break" and have never entertained the thought of establishing goals and structuring a plan to achieve them. They have no idea where they are going or how to get there.

As we explore each of the six basic areas of the Balance Wheel of Life, I would encourage you to consider what personal goals are important to you within each area. Write them down to reference later and possibly develop into full-blown goals.

Many people who hope to be successful are just waiting for their "big break" and have never entertained the thought of establishing goals and structuring a plan to achieve them.

SPIRITUAL

Within each one of us there is a dimension of our existence that is intangible, yet highly significant. This "spirit" life is expressed either through belief or unbelief in a supernatural power greater than ourselves. As we discussed in the previous chapter, our belief system shapes the fundamental perceptions (principles) of our lives. Those who do not believe in God will never enjoy the experience of transcending human activities. Those who do will be able to see their lives as a part of something much larger than themselves.

*The most
important goals
we can establish
are those that will
last an eternity.*

The truth is, we are all spiritual beings, made by the God of heaven and earth who created everything that exists. In fact, we were created in the very image of God, and it is only in Him that "we live and move and have our [very] being" (Acts 17:28). Through my own experiences, I have come to realize that true success in life can only be achieved by having an intimate relationship with God and His Son, Jesus Christ. Out of that relationship comes obedience to Him, and the inevitable result of obedience (which includes *doing* those things we know to do) is success in one form or another. The crucial thing is that everything we do should be based on our relationship with God.

As we plan and take action to achieve success, we have to remember that it is important to plan in accordance with the direction God gives us, because achievement and success in any other direction is hollow and will eventually prove meaningless. I mentioned my "rags to riches" story in the first chapter. When I became a millionaire at the age of twenty-three, my goals had not been based on direction from God. Because of the agony I experienced when I lost it all, I prayerfully turned to God as I began to change my goals to reflect His priorities and values.

The most important goals we can establish are those that will last an eternity. Even though it is important to set goals in the other five areas, spiritual goals are the only ones that will truly affect us and those around us forever. As you consider your spiritual goals, ask God to reveal His direction to you. Is reading through the Bible in a year a good goal for you? Perhaps your goal is to develop a servant's heart or to minister to others in some way with your time and/or finances. If you sense a real "longing" toward a certain area, that may be God speaking to your heart.

Without faith it is impossible to please God, because anyone who comes to him must believe that he exists and that he rewards those who earnestly seek him.

—HEBREWS 11:6

SOCIAL

Every aspect of our lives involves other people, but let's examine for just a moment those relationships that we form on a social level. The nature of each relationship will be different. Some will be smooth and pleasant; others will be difficult. Some will affect our lives significantly; others will be casual. Some will bring great meaning and purpose to our lives; others will be superficial. Our interactions with others occur in many different forms, but they occupy a huge portion of our lives.

It is important not to underestimate the profound influence relationships can have on every other area of our lives. The types of relationships and social activities we pursue deeply affect our spiritual lives. Our educational goals could be encouraged and supported by the people with whom we choose to spend time, or they could be undermined. Our families could be highly enriched by our choice of friends and activities, or they could be disappointed and unfulfilled. Friendships can even have a powerful influence on our eating habits, our commitment to exercise, our health and physical lives in general, and our financial goals. As we pursue balance in our social lives, it is important for those of us who are married to agree on common goals with our spouses. I have seen many married couples literally "stranded on the side of the road" in this area, because the husband spends most of his social time off fishing or playing golf with his buddies, rather than with his wife and family in pursuit of mutually beneficial relationships. Or the wife may be so involved in community or church activities that the family's time together is basically nonexistent. The lack of balance could simply be a matter of time: too much *or* too little time spent on certain activities.

Social activities are, by design, intended to provide rest and respite for our weary bodies and souls (our minds, wills, and emotions). The relationships and activities we choose can be tremendously uplifting and rewarding, providing a wonderful balance to the other five areas of our lives and contributing toward our success. Or, they can lead toward our eventual downfall and failure. When social relationships are out of balance, or when there is difficulty or turmoil in those relationships, our entire lives may seem out of control.

Spend some time with your family discussing the goals you want to set together. You can also set social goals that will meet your individual needs. Possible goals could include finding a new and interesting restaurant each month, meeting new friends, or inviting some close friends to your home for dinner once a month. Just be very aware that it is also easy to get "too busy" and not make time for this area of your life.

EDUCATIONAL

"An idle mind is the devil's workshop." While we all know this idiom is somewhat exaggerated, there is obviously much truth to it. The pursuit of knowledge is crucial to a healthy mind, and we must be in a constant state of learning if we want to achieve success.

The bottom line: If we have stopped learning, we have basically stopped living.

Someone once said, "Education is about one-tenth as costly as ignorance." The bottom line: If we have stopped learning, we have basically stopped living. Each new day presents endless opportunities to learn. Whether we want to pursue learning through formal education or through our own continuing education, we must constantly keep our minds open and alert to receive new information. Since much of the knowledge we possess came from other people at some point in our lives, part of our success depends on how much we are willing to learn from others.

The educational goals I have established in my own life are of great importance to me. I am constantly asking questions, watching, and listening to learn new things. I also read and/or study approximately 100 books a year. I listen to audiocassettes and watch educational television and videos. I *crave* knowledge (research, statistics, facts, and new ideas), because I know that without it I am doomed to a life of mediocrity.

Your educational goals may include obtaining a degree from a college or university, even though you already have a family and have been in the workforce for years. You may want to take classes or go to workshops to give you an edge in your existing job. Or you may want to attend a seminar or read a book on a subject about which you are passionate. As you pursue your educational goals, I encourage you to implement your newly found knowledge on a daily basis.

HOME AND FAMILY LIFE

To maintain balance and success in your family life, it is critical that you learn to be a good listener.

Our families are one of God's greatest gifts. We are charged with the responsibility of nurturing family relationships, with the overall goal of creating happy, secure, and successful families. The common threads of faithfulness and commitment hold successful families together, for those attributes create an atmosphere of love and trust in which families can thrive.

When we have difficulty, disagreement, or conflict in our family relationships, we can use those problems as learning tools to improve our relationships, or we can continue making the same mistakes. Through the generosity of time, we have the opportunity to mature and learn how to handle family relationships properly, or we can simply continue to wallow in the same mistakes and create more misery.

The Bible is the best practical handbook there is on personal and family relationships. Over and over we are encouraged to "fervently love one another from the heart" (1 Peter 1:22 NASB), to show "tolerance for one another in love" (Ephesians 4:2 NASB), and to "put on a heart of compassion, kindness, humility, gentleness, and patience; bearing with one another, and forgiving each other" (Colossians 3:12-13 NASB). Following these godly principles is the best insurance for having success-ful, happy families.

Another important key to good family relationships is good commu-nication. Most marriage counselors agree that one of the biggest problems in marriages is poor communication that results in erroneous perceptions. Some couples have gone for years believing they have been listening to each other, only to discover that real communication has never taken place. This is a potentially dangerous problem in any relationship. Children often complain that their parents don't understand them. Parents complain that their children don't listen to their advice.

To maintain balance and success in your family life, it is critical that you learn to be a good listener. An excellent way to test your listening skills is to sit down with someone in your family and work through the following exercise. You may want to choose someone with whom you have some difficulty communicating. Or, you may want to practice with your spouse, even if you believe you communicate well with each other. Schedule about thirty minutes with this person and find a comfortable, quiet place to talk.

Before you begin, review the guidelines for the conversation with your partner:

1. The subject of the conversation will be "Three things I would do right now with my life if money, time, and personal responsibilities were of no concern."

2. When your partner is speaking, you are not allowed to talk. You must listen until your partner says, "I have finished talking."

3. When your partner finishes speaking, repeat back to him or her *everything* you heard your partner say. When you have repeated what you think you heard, ask your partner, "Is that what you said?"

4. Your partner will then respond "yes" or "no." If the answer is "no," have your partner repeat what he or she said. After your partner has finished speaking, again repeat what you heard, leaving nothing out. Continue repeating this procedure until your partner agrees that you have repeated an exact rendition of everything he or she said.

This exercise is not intended to resolve issues, but to test listening skills. Actually, it can be fun! You may even end up communicating on a very deep level and improving the relationship. Whatever the case, you may discover in the process that your listening skills could use some work. Many times we think we hear something one way when it was intended quite differently. You may be amazed at how many times your partner will have to say something before you really "get it."

This simple exercise could have a huge impact on your family relationships. Effective listening skills are of critical importance to those who want to be successful over a long period of time. We need the help of others, especially those in our families, in order to be truly successful, and the more effectively we can communicate with others, the more effectively they can help.

What are some of your goals for your family and home life? To become a better listener? Perhaps you want to develop your children's self-esteem or establish a family devotion time for each day. Maybe your goal is to have a home that is peaceful, comfortable, and organized—one that is open and inviting to friends and extended family. Whatever your goals may be, investing in the lives of your family will produce immeasurable returns.

PHYSICAL AND HEALTH

If you could put a price tag on a healthy body, how much would it be? When we are young, none of us ever think we will suffer health

By setting goals that create and maintain a healthier body, you are taking steps that can literally benefit you for a lifetime!

problems; but we often fail to recognize the importance of developing healthy habits to ensure that we won't.

Even though nutritional products, health clubs, and exercise equipment sales have reached an all-time high in America, the population as a whole makes a very poor showing when it comes to having and maintaining good health. We may be doing whatever is required of us to achieve success in the other areas of our lives, but an open and honest self-evaluation probably would reveal that most of us are unbalanced in the area of physical well-being. I am afraid much of this problem stems from the fact that we, as Americans, are accustomed to having what we want when we want it and are not disciplined enough to pay the price for healthy bodies.

What good does it do to achieve success in other areas of our lives if we do not have the good health to enjoy our success? It is almost like putting on sunglasses to look at a beautiful sunset! Real success requires balance in *every* area of our lives, and the only way to appreciate our success is to stay healthy.

By setting goals that create and maintain a healthier body, you are taking steps that can literally benefit you for a lifetime! You may want to set a goal of joining a health club. Or perhaps scheduling a brisk evening walk (not just a leisurely stroll) with your spouse or your family is a good goal for you. By setting goals now, working toward them, and reaching them, you will be setting an example for your family and others to lead a healthier lifestyle.

FINANCIAL

How we handle our financial affairs is an indication of how well we are managing our lives. Making wise decisions and practicing good stewardship can affect the level of success we will achieve in other areas of our lives. Financial difficulties can often eventually be reversed, but our relationships, self-esteem, and peace of mind can be permanently damaged because of them. While a potential financial crisis or disaster cannot always be avoided, we still can set ourselves up for long-term financial success. By practicing a few sound principles of good stewardship, we can avoid many common pitfalls, prepare for unexpected needs, and be able to give to others.

While a potential financial crisis or disaster cannot always be avoided, we still can set ourselves up for long-term financial success.

The best way to determine how balanced we are in this part of our lives is to ask ourselves a simple question: *"Am I spending money primarily on my 'needs' or 'wants'?"* Obviously, needs and wants are in the eye of the beholder; but people who live their lives yielding to every compulsive want can experience a lifetime of frustration. I have experienced this frustration firsthand—since I have struggled with the temptation to give in to my "wants" frequently over the years. It is easy to get into the mode of compulsive buying, especially if we have the means to do so. Whenever I recognize that my habits are returning to a pattern of "want" spending, I have to step back and take measures to change my behavior.

A second question we can ask ourselves is, *"Am I giving something of myself and my time and finances to others?"* It is important to have a balanced view about our finances, and that includes giving some away to meet important needs in the lives of others. This is another indication of how well we are managing our lives. Are we in tune with God and giving back to Him as He gives to us? Are we generous in our relationships and interaction with others? Do we freely give to our family (with common sense and wisdom)?

Did you know that God wants to bless you in every area of your life—including your finances? God loves to give us good things, just as we love to bless our own children. If you have difficulty believing that God really wants to bless you, I would recommend that you read a wonderful little book called *The Prayer of Jabez* by Bruce Wilkinson. Wilkinson points out a tiny portion of Scripture—only two verses—that contain a powerful message:

> *Now Jabez was more honorable than his brothers, and his mother called his name Jabez, saying, "Because I bore him in*

pain." And Jabez called on the God of Israel saying, "Oh, that You would bless me indeed, and enlarge my territory, that Your hand would be with me, and that You would keep me from evil, that I may not cause pain!" So God granted him what he requested.

—1 CHRONICLES 4:9-10 NKJV

Wilkinson does a great job of bringing practical application to this prayer and gives testimonial proof that God does, indeed, love to bless us. This concept is so powerful that I buy the book by the hundreds and give it away. My point is threefold: (1) Jabez was more honorable than his brothers (he was in right standing with God); (2) he prayed for blessings; and (3) God granted what he requested. It is not wrong to pray for blessings—it is what we do with those blessings that determines whether we maintain balance in the area of financial matters.

The very first step toward financial success is goal setting. Becoming debt free might be one of the first goals you set for yourself and your family. College funds for your children might be another goal. When you write down your financial goals, be sure to consider such things as where you are currently spending your money, potential business opportunities, desired monthly income, and ways that you might like to give.

"We make a living by what we get, we make a life by what we give."

—SIR WINSTON CHURCHILL

MANAGING OUR LIVES

Success is only achieved through the effective use of our time and resources and by finding the right balance within each of the six areas of life (spiritual, social, educational, home and family life, physical and health, and financial). The daily management of these areas must be rooted and grounded in our relationship with God, and no one component should dominate, distort, or overpower the others. There will be occasions when we may purposely be out of balance in a certain area of our lives if that area needs special attention—say in times of a family emergency or a financial crisis. However, the key is to recognize and understand how balancing these components affects our personal achievement and success.

Consistency is the best measurement of a well-managed life, and time is the great equalizing factor that establishes a demanding reality for each of us. It is said that we can all experience our fifteen minutes of fame, but the test of real achievement must be held in the balance of an entire life. In other words, through the years and during the significant events of our lives a pattern will begin to emerge. If we are seeking real achievement and success, our choices and decisions should consistently have a positive effect on all six areas of our lives.

"Life is a great big canvas; throw all the paint you can at it."

—DANNY KAYE

None of us can go through life without experiencing failure in one area or another. But if there is positive consistency in our lives (that is, if we consistently learn from our mistakes and mature through them to bring harmony and balance to our lives), we can, for the most part, avoid repeating the same mistakes. Time is the vehicle that allows us to make course corrections, and time allows us to recover and improve. High achievers will see the future as an endless opportunity because of all they can learn and accomplish—rather than seeing doom and disaster because of missed opportunities and what "might have been" in the past.

Perhaps while reading this chapter you have identified some areas in your life that are out of balance. Maybe your spiritual life is lacking, and you want a deeper relationship with God. Perhaps you have a family relationship that is suffering. You may be experiencing a crisis in your financial matters. Or you may realize that there is no positive consistency in your life. It is important for you to know that, no matter how difficult your situation may be right now, as long as there is breath, there is *hope*. Time is on your side, and you can change. Setting new goals in each area of your life will go a long way toward the achievement of real success.

VIPs
(VERY IMPORTANT POINTS)

⚑ Those who lack good life-management skills will have difficulty sustaining the discipline needed to produce continued success.

⚑ Consistent discipline will continually move you toward success as you set your goals, make your plans to reach them, and work to accomplish your objectives.

⚑ The relationships and activities we choose can be tremendously uplifting and rewarding or they can lead toward our eventual downfall and failure.

⚑ Since much of the knowledge we possess came from other people at some point in our lives, part of our success depends on how much we are willing to learn from others.

⚑ Success is achieved only through the effective use of our time and resources and by finding the right balance within each of the six areas of life.

3

A WINNING ATTITUDE

When I was just seventeen years old, I set a significant goal for myself: to become a millionaire by the time I was twenty-five. Even at that young age, somehow I *knew* I could achieve that goal. I had a winning attitude.

I had already achieved some unusual accomplishments for someone my age, which helped produce confidence in myself and my abilities. Working three jobs, including a successful lawn business, I had already established credit and purchased a house, trading repair and restoration work for the down payment. I owned three cars by my senior year in high school, two of which were paid for free and clear.

Determination and persistence propelled me toward my goal. Many people laughed at me because of my dream, but I stayed focused on my objective and constantly

These three components— confidence, persistence, and enthusiasm—are key ingredients required for a winning attitude, which is the engine of achievement.

listened to motivational tapes and read success books. One major influence was the book *How to Win Friends and Influence People* by Dale Carnegie, which really encouraged me to be persistent about achieving my dream! Of course, it didn't hurt that I grew up in a supportive family of entrepreneurs who encouraged self-discipline. The reason I had a flourishing lawn business as a teenager was because I had carefully watched my grandfather and my father take good care of their customers. They modeled "customer service" and "doing more than is expected" for me, and I worked hard to follow the same business principles that had made them successful.

And I was *excited!* My enthusiasm fueled my daily activities. I wrote and reviewed my goals on a regular basis, and virtually every day I made lists of the things I needed to accomplish to achieve my goal.

Imagine how excited I was when I reached my goal—two years early!

These three components—confidence, persistence, and enthusiasm—are key ingredients required for a winning attitude, which is the engine of achievement. Having a winning attitude is the third pillar in the foundation for accelerated success. Success cannot be attained without winning—and winning consistently. Since it is important to understand what winning is all about, let's start with a good definition.

The Merriam-Webster dictionary defines a *winner* as:

> *"One that is successful especially through praiseworthy ability and hard work."*

According to our definition, to be a winner requires hard work. We have already determined that success means accomplishing something that was planned for in advance. Winning is the first cousin of success, since winning is the point when a planned goal is actually completed (success) and rewards are received as a result of the effort.

Unfortunately, winning is often associated with a contest of some kind, or a competition that produces a winner—and a loser. With this perception, many people approach life as a contest between themselves and everyone else. They believe that in order to "win" and get ahead, their coworkers or any perceived "competition" must lose. Others may have subconsciously processed through their belief windows that winning in life may be rude, perhaps even cruel. The above definition clearly proves that winning can be an individual activity that does not necessarily leave losers in its wake.

Do nothing out of selfish ambition or vain conceit, but in humility consider others better than yourselves. Each of you should look not only to your own interests, but also to the interests of others.

—PHILIPPIANS 2:3-4

The dividends of winning can be both tangible and intangible. Winning can produce money, material possessions, goodwill, and even wisdom—none of which has to be obtained by taking anything from another person. Of course, honest competition is sometimes necessary, and the "loser" may feel a sense of loss; but winning in life involves pure reward for purely motivated effort, and it can be done without hurting a soul.

It is a false belief that in order to achieve success an individual must and should trample upon everyone who "stands in his way." Success is the achievement of personal goals and should never involve intentionally hurting someone else. In fact, sometimes the greatest success can be measured by the number of people we influence and encourage in their own pursuit of success. Why not help someone else achieve *his* goals while you are pursuing yours? In the pursuit of true success, winning is a *good* thing, and its rewards are most enjoyable when shared with others.

Since having a winning attitude is so important for achieving success, we must become entirely comfortable with the concept if we want to quicken personal achievement. We must understand the true definition of "winning" and give ourselves permission to be successful. A person who does not have the zeal to win won't! It is that simple.

True winners see things as they really are, whether good or bad, and choose to respond with confidence, persistence, and enthusiasm!

CONFIDENCE + PERSISTENCE + ENTHUSIASM = WINNING ATTITUDE

Since a winning attitude is the engine of achievement, let's examine the three cardinal elements of a winning attitude: confidence, persistence, and enthusiasm.

A person with a winning attitude, or a positive attitude, is *not* someone who goes through life denying reality and looking at everything through rose-colored glasses. On the contrary, people who are true winners see things as they really are, whether good or bad, and choose to respond with confidence, persistence, and enthusiasm! A positive attitude is not an act, a gimmick, or a magic formula to be taken out and used at will. It must be developed and practiced until it becomes a natural response.

I can do all things
in him who
strengthens me.

—PHILIPPIANS
4:13 RSV

WHAT IS CONFIDENCE?

Let's look at another definition from Merriam-Webster:

Confident: 1: characterized by assurance, especially: SELF-RELIANT; 3a: full of conviction: CERTAIN; b: COCKSURE.

People who have confidence *know* they can do whatever it is that has to be done. Their confidence is an attitude about life itself—a certain optimism about themselves and their overall abilities. Confident people have developed their self-assurance over a period of time by proving certain things to themselves from their own experiences, namely that they can usually do anything they need to do if they devote enough time, effort, and energy to the task at hand. Confident people are not afraid to try new things or take reasonable risks. How does one achieve this sense

Experience,

accomplishments,

knowledge, and

understanding

all work together

to produce

confidence—and

competence as well.

of optimism? Obviously, no one is born with confidence. I believe it is acquired through a process.

In Chapter One, we discussed our windows of belief that contain all that we believe to be true. Our confidence comes from the things we believe about ourselves, and it either grows or diminishes with the results we achieve and the attitudes of the people with whom we associate. I have found that periodically reminding myself of my achievements, whether large or small, is the most powerful confidence builder I can employ.

When I was a young Cub Scout, I entered the Pinewood Derby. My dad and I worked diligently on the design of my car, and I carved, painted, and polished it to near perfection. Because of all my preparation, I was confident that I would win—and I did! To this day, thirty years later, I keep that car in my office in plain sight as a reminder of what hard work can accomplish—and it continues to build my confidence.

Another practice that has proved helpful for me is keeping the letters I receive from my clients close at hand. Reading these letters often gives me confidence, particularly when they express great satisfaction with my work. However, I also make note of the feedback these letters provide, so that I am better able to plan to meet their needs and produce the desired results the next time I work with them. Because of these reminders, I approach each day and each task with a great amount of confidence that I will be successful.

Often, there is a certain expected progression of confidence building associated with age. Young people just out of college normally have little experience and are expected to work for less than those with more experience. People in their mid-forties are believed to be in their "prime" and are considered to be more valuable assets. They also earn more money. What happened to these people between the ages of twenty-one and forty-five? They gained experience, and hopefully they accumulated some accomplishments and gained a good bit of knowledge and understanding. Experience, accomplishments, knowledge, and understanding all work together to produce confidence—and competence as well.

On the other hand, there are some people in their mid-forties who have made little progress in the area of confidence. They don't seem to have much more knowledge than they did at twenty-one, and their lack of achievement may have become a source of bitterness and discontent. They often feel left behind.

What is the difference between these two groups of people? Obviously, age and time alone are not the main ingredients of confidence. I believe there is a cyclical relationship between confidence and winning experiences. Each is reinforced by the other. As we experience one, we grow in the other. The more winning experiences we have, the greater our confidence level. And the greater our confidence, the more "wins" we will experience.

BACK TO THE FUTURE

Sometimes movies can be good illustrations of these important life principles. In *Back to the Future*, Michael J. Fox stars as the son of parents who were underachievers in life. His father was a timid soul who seemed to avoid achievement in any form. When Michael was propelled back in time to the fifties, he had the opportunity to meet his parents as teenagers and became involved in setting his parents up on their first date. It was on that date that his father was confronted by a bully and challenged to defend his honor and protect the girl who would later become his wife and Michael's mother.

In the original event Michael's father had failed, and the bully had won. During the "replay," his father found confidence and triumphed over the bully, with Michael's help. The results of this small alteration in history were momentous. When Michael went "back to the future," his entire family had changed. His father was a successful author, and both his parents were energetic participants in life. The "bully" was a timid individual who dropped by from time to time to wash and wax their cars. The change in that one event completely altered the lives of his parents.

This is a fictional example, of course, but there are untold numbers of stories about real people whose lives have been changed when they experienced a turning point that gave them newfound confidence. Can you think of an example from your own life? In my book *Designing Your Own Life,* I present an exercise that encourages people to think about their lives and create a list of all their accomplishments—great and small. Most people never do that; and when they see everything they have accomplished in life on one list, it can be shocking. The result is that they gain confidence.

In his book, *The Best Seller,* Ron Willingham says that lack of confidence is often caused by fear. He explains that when the Apostle John writes that "perfect love drives out fear" (1 John 4:18), the love referred to is that love that seeks the highest good for others. When you want the best for those you are serving, you become less self-centered and more focused on others. You lose your fear of rejection, appear more professional, and "persuade with the highest form of persuasion—integrity!" The result is confidence!

When it comes to personal achievement, there may be nothing more important than confidence. Confidence gives us the ability to experience new things and to take chances. When people are confident, it is exuded in their attitudes and is visible to others.

PERSISTENCE

An individual who is persistent continues to do something in a determined way, even in the face of difficulties or opposition. Winning requires persistence. This is the hard part of the equation, because there

There is one thing certain about quitting: People who quit will not finish, and if they don't finish, they will not win!

is nothing more difficult than pressing on in spite of something negative that has happened, mistakes that have been made, or any number of other obstacles that can present a temptation to quit. Quitting is not an option.

Zig Ziglar tells a story about going to his health club to work out during the first week of January and finding the place so packed he had a hard time finding a parking space. When he got inside, equipment use was at an all-time high. He inquired with the manager about the reason for the crowd and was told, "Oh, this is just the New Year's resolution crowd. Most of them will be gone in a month or two."

Unfortunately, people usually begin more things than they finish. There is one thing certain about quitting: People who quit will not finish, and if they don't finish, they will not win! Nothing about success is certain except the result of quitting—it will guarantee failure every time. Unfortunately, human beings are masters at coming up with good, logical reasons for quitting, because they usually do not want to admit that they simply gave up!

There is a certain quality a person must have to create persistence and press on when circumstances become difficult. This quality, desire, is the fuel of persistence! To have the courage to overcome obstacles and difficulties, a person has to "want to." If you are motivated to achieve success and are setting new personal goals, it is helpful to take inventory of your "want to" factors. Your answers to the following questions should reveal your level of desire:

1. Do you have a clear understanding of your reasons for setting this new goal?

2. Have you carefully considered the potential ramifications and benefits?

3. Have you anticipated the potential situations that might tempt you to quit?

4. Are you doing this for yourself, or only for someone else?

5. Do you think you will enjoy doing what you want to do?

If the answer to three or more of these questions is "yes," chances are you have a good level of "want to" and will have success in completing your goals. If three or more of these questions are answered with a "no," you probably aren't really sure what you want to achieve, and the odds are high that you will quit before you reach your goals. The honest level of desire to do something is very important and must be considered any time you begin a new project or activity. The chances of finishing are excellent if you are confident and really want to do it.

ENTHUSIASM

When we are enthusiastic about doing something, we are inspired to accomplish it. Enthusiasm is another natural by-product of desire, and our level of enthusiasm is the final test for determining whether we have a winning environment that will help us achieve accelerated success. Lack of enthusiasm reveals a lack of desire; and as we have already discussed, a person who does not have the desire to win probably won't.

Certainly, we are not always excited about the demands made on us by our personal and professional lives. But enthusiasm is something that naturally flows out of us when we are 100 percent committed to what we are striving to accomplish. I don't believe real enthusiasm can be counterfeited. However, if we are doing something we know we must do to be successful, and we aren't entirely enthusiastic about it, there is no reason to despair. There is hope! In fact, we can probably find the answer by simply returning to the first point discussed in this chapter: *confidence!*

These three crucial elements of a winning attitude are tightly interwoven: confidence, persistence, and enthusiasm. I believe confidence is the most essential element because we don't have to be enthusiastic to be confident. Neither do we have to be persistent to be confident. But we do have to be confident to maintain persistence, and we need confidence to be enthusiastic. That is why I believe we should work on our confidence level if we are not as enthusiastic as we ought to be.

We can always develop greater confidence by learning from our experiences and by studying and practicing in order to become more competent. The real benefit is, once we have acquired confidence, we have laid a good foundation for persistence and enthusiasm.

It is very important to remember that we need help from others if we are to succeed, and our enthusiasm—or lack of it—will either inspire and encourage others, or dishearten and discourage them.

We are normally not too thrilled about buying something from a salesperson who is not enthusiastic about his or her product. If we aren't enthusiastic about what we are doing, our lack of confidence will have the same effect on the people we may need to help us. Enthusiasm is contagious, and it generates credibility that attracts other people.

A winning attitude shows. It is an absolute requirement for success. It is not positive thinking—it is confident, persistent, and enthusiastic thinking. There is no stopping a person with such an attitude!

VIPs
(VERY IMPORTANT POINTS)

⚑ Three components—confidence, persistence, and enthusiasm—are key ingredients required for a winning attitude, which is the engine of achievement.

⚑ Sometimes the greatest success can be measured by the number of people we influence and encourage in their own pursuit of success.

⚑ True winners see things as they really are, whether good or bad, and choose to respond with confidence, persistence, and enthusiasm!

⚑ Experience, accomplishments, knowledge, and understanding all work together to produce confidence—and competence as well.

Section Two:

STRATEGIES

4

SUCCESS REQUIRES ACTION!

We have discussed the three pillars in the foundation of success: embracing *right* principles in our belief windows, maintaining a well-balanced life, and developing a winning attitude. On that solid foundation, we are now ready to build the strategies for success: taking the necessary action; maximizing effectiveness; and planning, goal setting, and speed.

At this point, we need to establish a good definition of success. I believe that success is a process, not an event, and that some rewards are produced as a result of the process. The rewards may be tangible (houses, cars, luxury items, etc.), but success also produces even more important results that are often less tangible, such as strong families, peace of mind, stability, and good relationships.

"The dictionary is the only place where success comes before work."

—MARK TWAIN

Let's look first at how *success* is defined in some of the world's great dictionaries:

Webster's 1828 Dictionary:

The favorable or prosperous termination of any thing attempted.

Webster's Unabridged Dictionary 1913:

That which comes after; hence, consequence, issue, or result, of an endeavor or undertaking, whether good or bad; the outcome of effort.

The Wordsmyth Education Dictionary-Thesaurus:

The attainment of something desired or intended.

American Heritage® Dictionary of the English Language:

The achievement of something desired, planned, or attempted.

We are successful when we are able to consistently accomplish predetermined, written goals and motivate positive actions in other people that support, complement, and enhance our goals.

You may have noticed that these definitions of success progress chronologically from how the term was perceived in 1828 to the way it is defined in the present day. Even though they span a period of almost two hundred years, the definitions are essentially the same, and they all have two distinct parts: the first speaks of planning to do something, and the second involves actually taking the action to achieve a desired result.

I would like to give you my own definition of success. I believe we are successful when we are able to *consistently accomplish predetermined, written goals and motivate positive actions in other people that support, complement, and enhance our goals.* If we can repeatedly accomplish this, we will usually attain the tangible and intangible rewards we desire.

Notice the word "predetermined." The planning process is an essential part of success—it requires planning *and* action. Most people have trouble connecting these two critical requirements. They may have a genuine longing to be successful, but either they are unwilling to plan for success, or they are unwilling to take the necessary action to execute their plans. Yes, dreams and vision are required before one can be successful; but success occurs only when a plan is created to make those dreams and vision a reality and the necessary steps are taken to bring them to fruition.

Another reason many individuals are not successful is they can get stuck in a pattern of repeating actions that don't work. It is not enough to simply act; it must be the *right* action. Many people have made big plans and made an effort to accomplish their plans, but they have never been successful. Something always seems to happen to sabotage their efforts, and they never quite reach the brass ring. You may have had some experiences like that in your own life. I certainly did, until I discovered a few basic truths and put them into practice.

> *"That some achieve great success is proof to all that others can achieve it as well."*
>
> —ABRAHAM LINCOLN

For many years I have read the great works of success and personal achievement experts. As I studied and began to put many of their success principles into action, I discovered that a significant key to success is to begin with a *good* plan and then take the *correct* action. The plan must be realistic, and the action steps to accomplish the plan must actually produce the desired result. Without the diligence to plan and the discipline to follow through, it is almost impossible to reach a pinnacle of success. In order to achieve success and fulfill our God-given destiny, we must be consistent and relentless in our pursuit.

A significant key to success is to begin with a good plan and then take the correct action.

This pursuit demands a great deal of mental focus and emotional energy. As we established in Chapter One, the principles in our belief windows actually lay the foundation for and control our actions. An individual who has been unsuccessful at implementing his plan may need to change his thought processes, beginning with the principles in his window. Change is very difficult and can often be painful. But it is the willingness to change that is the key to success acceleration. A person cannot keep doing the same things over and over and expect different results.

UNDERSTANDING WHY WE DO WHAT WE DO

The reasons we do the things we do are not always obvious. Since action is such an important part of success, it is imperative that we understand how our thinking controls the choices we make and the actions we take.

Understanding and accepting that the things we do may be hindering our success enables us to change our actions and therefore quicken the art of personal achievement. Changing our actions usually involves passing through four stages of awareness and competence. Let's follow the process through the model using a bicycle as an example:

Stage 1: Unconscious Incompetence. We are all born with unconscious incompetence. That simply means that we "don't know that we don't know." For example, at that point we have never seen or heard about bicycles, but we don't realize that we don't know anything about bicycles. We would be incompetent about the ability to ride a bicycle, but we wouldn't know that we were incompetent.

Stage 2: Conscious Incompetence. In this stage, we are aware of the fact that we don't know, but we still lack the ability to accomplish the task. Using the bicycle again as an illustration, it would mean that we are aware of how much fun a bicycle can be, but we still do not know how to ride one.

Stage 3: Conscious Competence. In this stage, we have begun to take some action to overcome our incompetence in the area of

Understanding and accepting that the things we do may be hindering our success enables us to change our actions and therefore quicken the art of personal achievement.

bikes, but we still have to work at it—and it's not easy. Perhaps someone has given us some lessons on how to ride a bike, but we still have to think carefully about everything we do while we are on the bicycle.

Stage 4: Unconscious Competence. During this stage, the action we take to accomplish the task in question is second nature to us. We know our subject—in this case, bicycles—and have practiced long enough to operate one with little thought or effort. At this stage we don't have to think about how to ride the bike. We just get on it, and the entire riding process is automatic. We keep our balance without thinking about it. We pedal the bike without thinking. The bike is a part of us, and we are a part of the bike. We are unconsciously competent. We can ride a bicycle without giving it a thought.

It is important to understand these four stages of competence, because success and achievement work the same way. If we are unconsciously incompetent about goal setting, for example, we can't expect to be successful. If we are to achieve success, we must first realize our unconscious incompetence about goals and then achieve at least the stage of conscious competence until we have become a competent goal setter. As we journey toward success, every principle and task required in the process will move us through these four stages of competence. In other words, change is inevitable!

GOAL SETTING

Once again, our definition of success is *the ability to consistently accomplish predetermined, written goals and create positive actions in other people* that support, complement, and enhance our goals. Please notice that the whole *process* of success begins with goal setting. We will discuss this subject in greater detail in Chapter Six, but I want to emphasize here that *nothing happens* until we set our sights on where we want to go. Success requires *action*, and our goals are the only road map we have to show us what actions to take to get there.

I began the process of becoming a serious goal-setter about twenty years ago. Since that time, I have fine-tuned the process into a system that has allowed me to accomplish 80 to 90 percent of all the goals I have set for myself. I am convinced that I have been able to enjoy this measure of success because I have incorporated three key elements every time I set a goal:

1. I set realistic goals that stretch me but are achievable.

2. I review and thoroughly evaluate the progress of my goals at least four times a year.

3. I share my goals with others and seek their help and assistance.

Setting realistic goals that are within reach is doubly important, not only because *I* have to believe they can be accomplished, but also

"Flaming enthusiasm, backed by horse sense and persistence, is the quality that most frequently makes for success."

—DALE CARNEGIE

because when I share them with others to solicit their assistance, *they* have to believe they are realistic as well. By thoroughly reviewing my goals at least four times a year, I can make course corrections for even greater opportunity along the way, and I am able to stay on top of my progress. A regular review of my goals also makes me accountable to myself. It is difficult for anyone to have a successful goals program without accountability. However, it is the third key, sharing my goals with others, that has had the biggest impact on my ability to accomplish my goals.

I can't accomplish a thing without the help of others! By sharing my goals with people in a position to help me, I increase the odds that the actions they take will be pointed in the right direction. This approach has produced consistent results for me over a long period of time.

> *"The most important thing in communication is to hear what isn't being said."*
>
> —PETER F. DRUCKER

I am equally interested in other people's goals. I need to know what they want to accomplish so I can help them more effectively. I have a detailed understanding of the personal goals of the people with whom I work and associate. In truth, some have been somewhat reluctant to present their goals to me. But because this concept is so important to me, I have been persistent, even if I have had to sometimes "drag" the information out of them. Knowing each other's goals enables us to work together more effectively and builds a strong, supportive relationship with one another.

As we walked through the six elements of a well-managed life in Chapter Two, you may have noticed that I made suggestions for setting effective goals in each area. As I achieve goals in each of the six areas of my life, I set new ones! Success is a process, and I never want to stop "being successful!"

You can consistently achieve success as well. Identify your goals, establish a *good* plan, take the *right* actions, and you are well on your way!

VIPs
(VERY IMPORTANT POINTS)

- We are successful when we are able to consistently accomplish predetermined, written goals and motivate positive actions in other people that support, complement, and enhance our goals.

- A significant key to success is to begin with a *good* plan and then take the *correct* action.

- Many individuals are not successful because they can get stuck in a pattern of repeating actions that don't work. It is not enough to simply act; it must be the *right* action.

- Understanding and accepting that the things we do may be hindering our success enables us to change our actions and therefore quicken the art of personal achievement.

- Sharing our goals with those around us enables us all to work together more effectively and build stronger, supportive relationships.

5

MAXIMIZING PERSONAL EFFECTIVENESS

The strategies we have discussed thus far have emphasized the importance of taking action and completing things. The very concept of success we embrace is based on accomplishing specific things we have planned to do. The key word here is *planned!* And the sole result we seek from planning is to be effective. As Steven Covey says, "Begin with the end in mind."

THE EFFECTIVENESS PACKAGE

Success acceleration can't happen without some personal effort. Effective people make things happen and consistently get the results they want to achieve. Their lives typically demonstrate five characteristics:

1.   Effective people accept responsibility.

2.   Effective people get results.

3.   Effective people are energetic.

4. Effective people are competent.

5. Effective people are open to correcting principles in their belief windows.

The above characteristics make up what might well be called the "effectiveness package." Those who demonstrate these characteristics will no doubt achieve results consistently, and those who are weak in any of these areas will experience little effectiveness.

As we discuss each of these characteristics, those who want to cultivate effectiveness in themselves should be asking:

1. Does this characteristic describe me?

2. Is this characteristic a strength or a shortcoming?

3. How can I improve in this area?

4. Are there five things I do regularly that demonstrate this characteristic in my life?

> *Happy is the man who finds wisdom, and the man who gets understanding, for the gain from it is better than gain from silver and its profit better than gold.*
>
> —PROVERBS 3:13-14 RSV

A PORTRAIT OF EFFECTIVENESS

First and foremost, highly effective people *accept responsibility* for their own actions and do not make excuses for failure.

In so doing, they invoke respect and admiration from their families, their friends, and their professional associates. I believe there is no quality more admired than that of refusing to "pass the buck." Accepting responsibility demonstrates courage, honesty, and trustworthiness. Those who posses this quality attract others who want to help them be successful, which is a crucial necessity for consistent achievement.

A person who denies responsibility often cannot see things as they really are and will most often fail at whatever he or she is attempting to do. If we are to achieve and be effective, we must constantly learn from our mistakes and grow in our abilities and understanding.

Second, effective people love to *get results*. They thrive on production, not useless activity, and they understand that focused action is the way things are accomplished.

They know the difference between "busy" activities and activities that produce results. They are action-oriented, proactive people who seek solutions. They know that failure often follows procrastination, so they don't "hunker down" in defensive positions and wait for the right time or the right opportunity! *Fortune Magazine* recently published an article that told about thirty-four CEOs of top companies in the nation who were terminated because of their failure to produce results. This is a powerful demonstration of the importance of effectiveness.

The third characteristic of effective people, which is closely related to being action-oriented, is being *energetic*. If a person does not possess a high level of energy, it is difficult for him to maintain consistent activity.

An energetic person has the intensity, the persistence, and the prolonged stamina to accomplish long-term goals. This kind of energy involves an observable determination that is always present—a constant striving to accomplish whatever it is the person is trying to achieve. It stems from a strong belief in what the person is attempting to accomplish and a passionate commitment to do it.

The fourth element of effectiveness is *competence.* Competent people are effective because they have acquired the skills they need to perform the tasks they undertake. Those who hope to maximize their effectiveness must give consideration to the skills needed to achieve their goals. Achievement demands competence.

Finally, effective people are *open to correcting principles in their belief windows.* They embrace those principles they believe to be rock-solid, but they are open to new concepts and ideas that prove worthy. They invite and encourage advice from trusted colleagues and are not hesitant to incorporate new ways of doing things to achieve timely results. Change is not a bad thing in the eyes of effective people. They validate the results, make adjustments as necessary, and continually look for better and faster ways to get a job done.

Most people possess varying amounts of these five characteristics of effectiveness. The important thing is to be aware that they are an essential part of the strategy to achieve long-term success. I encourage you to use the chart below to rate your own strengths in these critical areas:

	Critical Factors	Strengths
1.	EFFECTIVE PEOPLE ACCEPT RESPONSIBILITY.	1 2 3 4 5 6 7 8 9 10
2.	EFFECTIVE PEOPLE GET RESULTS.	1 2 3 4 5 6 7 8 9 10
3.	EFFECTIVE PEOPLE ARE ENERGETIC.	1 2 3 4 5 6 7 8 9 10
4.	EFFECTIVE PEOPLE ARE COMPETENT.	1 2 3 4 5 6 7 8 9 10
5.	EFFECTIVE PEOPLE ARE OPEN TO CORRECTING PRINCIPLES IN THEIR WINDOWS OF BELIEF.	1 2 3 4 5 6 7 8 9 10

TIME

The five qualities of effectiveness can all be demonstrated within the framework of something we simply call "time." All have a close relationship to time and the way time is used. People who accept responsibility are prompt in carrying out their actions. Results-oriented people do things focused on completion. Energetic people try to get as much done as possible within each hour. Competent people have the skills to manage their time and rarely miss deadlines. Finally, people who are open to making adjustments in their belief windows know how to work outside the box to get the job done in short amounts of time. Effective people have learned how to balance their energy and action against the clock so they don't burn out in a short period of time. They understand the nature of time and how to use it wisely.

Time is an asset. In fact, it may be our most valuable asset. A unique thing about time is that it is universally fair. Everyone starts each day with the same amount of time, and they choose how they will use it. The choices we make about using our time will be driven by the five characteristics of effectiveness just discussed.

Major corporations have invested millions of dollars in personal planning systems and time-management seminars to help their people better manage their time. Although these are great tools, I have made a few observations about time management that may be a bit shocking.

> *Effective people manage their time effectively because they have the principle in their belief windows that time is important.*

If we were to survey 500 people in a company who had all begun using sophisticated time-management systems at the same time, we would hope they all had become highly productive people who never wasted any time. However, in our experience, we have found that after a year or two such people are still doing things the way they always did them. Those who were always late for meetings are still late for meetings. The people who missed project deadlines still miss them. Those who were always on time are still arriving on time, and the people who were always dependable are still dependable. The point is that the tools we use are only as effective as we are.

People who have a great number of strengths in the five characteristics of effectiveness will use time to their advantage. A person who does not possess a modicum of these five characteristics could carry half a dozen time-management systems around with him and still be lost. It is interesting to note in a meeting attended by a number of people who all bring their personal planners that some of those planners are never opened and some appear to be nothing more than eight-pound calendars. It is not the tool that determines the effectiveness—it is the mind-set.

Effective people know how to manage their time, and they can do it with sophisticated time-management systems, or they can do it with nothing more than a legal pad. They manage their time effectively because they have the principle in their belief windows that time is important. They usually live by the question my good friend Brian Tracy teaches, "What is the best use of my time *right now?*" They understand the value of time, and they know it is not an asset to be squandered.

People who are willing to look honestly at how they manage their time will be able to determine their level of effectiveness. Results and day-to-day behavior are the real proof of time management. Answers to

"Action springs not
from thought, but
from a readiness for
responsibility."

—DIETRICH
BONHOEFFER

the questions below will determine how well you are performing in this critical area.

1. *What time do you start each day?* Effective people don't spend half the day in bed. Unless they are in a specialized profession that requires unusual working hours, the most effective people normally start their days early. In the sales profession, it is a well-known fact that the best time to reach a decision-maker on the phone is early in the morning. Many top executives arrive at work long before their staffs and have even been known to answer an early phone call themselves. Effective people realize the true value of starting their day early.

2. *Are you an "on-time" person?* When you keep appointments and attend meetings, do you arrive on time, every time? Unavoidable things may detain people occasionally, but those who maximize their time are rarely late. Ninety-nine percent of the time, being late is a result of poor planning. If you have a tendency to be habitually late, you should examine this area closely. You may want to just adjust your mental clock to "Vince Lombardi time," which is always twenty minutes early.

3. *When you have a project to do, how much time to you spend "getting ready" before you start?* Obviously, a certain amount of

preparation is necessary to properly organize any project; but there is a point when preparation can become procrastination and avoidance. Planning is important, but when it goes on too long, the amount of time that is wasted can be enormous. The key here is to get started at the right time, with the right degree of preparation. If you really want an honest opinion about your tendency toward procrastination, you may want to ask someone you trust—perhaps even your boss! Bosses are the ones generating the work, and they are the ones most likely to have an opinion. If you are self-employed, you may want to ask a trusted client.

4. *What are your top three time-wasting activities?* To answer this question, it may be necessary to reflect on your activities at the end of each day for several days, looking at your "to do" list, Day-Timer™, Palm Pilot™, or any other time-management tool you use. Try to remember any activities that were not particularly productive; just by looking at the top three nonproductive items, you should be able to determine how much time was lost.

5. *Do you scramble to meet deadlines?* This last question may be the most important. There are usually dates established for completing projects or accomplishing goals. If you always end up having to do 90 percent of the work in 30 percent of the allotted time, it is a reflection of how you spend your time. If you have difficulty meeting deadlines, you probably need to change the way you manage your time. When a project is late, the time

cannot be redeemed. Some people are continually forced to push items on their "to do" lists into the future that should have been accomplished that day. Some things will always have to be rescheduled, but rescheduling should not be a way of life. Deadlines should be met on a consistent basis. It is important to focus on completion! I do my best to complete things ahead of schedule; to be ready physically and mentally for what might come next. This enables me to be ready for the next opportunity and exceed expectations.

BE MORE EFFECTIVE

Getting things done and accomplishing results are the proof of success. A person who wants to be more effective must acquire or improve the five characteristics of effective people. The amazing thing is that the use of a person's time will improve in direct relationship to the acquisition and application of the five characteristics. Let's review those characteristics again:

Effective people accept responsibility.

Effective people get results.

Effective people are energetic.

Effective people are competent.

Effective people are open to making adjustments in their belief windows.

People who possess these qualities rarely waste time. They remain focused and committed to the completion of projects, and they demand results from themselves and others.

Virtually every successful person has a plan or a blueprint for the actions he wants to take, and this preplanning requires the development of a strong strategy. Strategy focuses on the methods, processes, or techniques that will be used to support the plan.

Developing a strategy involves looking at assets (the five characteristics of effectiveness) and determining how they will be deployed. Nothing dilutes achievement like wasting time and energy. Those who hope to maximize their effectiveness must maximize the use of their time.

VIPs

(VERY IMPORTANT POINTS)

- Highly effective people accept responsibility for their own actions and do not make excuses for failure.

- Those who hope to maximize their effectiveness must give consideration to the skills needed to achieve their goals. Achievement demands competence.

- Successful people manage their time effectively because they have the principle in their belief windows that time is important.

- Virtually every successful person has a plan or a blueprint for the actions he wants to take, and this preplanning requires the development of a strong strategy.

6

PLANNING, GOAL SETTING, AND SPEED

My interest in success began very early in life as I watched my grandfather run a successful family business. From the time I bought the business from him when I was seventeen until today, I have set and refined my goals virtually every quarter of every year. That means they have had over two decades of refinement. My current goals binder now consists of some eighty-five pages. I have written a book, *Designing Your Own Life*, based on my personal system, and I teach workshops on the same subject.

I have also learned valuable lessons about success from failure, because, like most entrepreneurs, I have not been completely successful in all of my ventures. Some endeavors have been disastrous, to say the least. However, I have a principle in my belief window that I have made a Standard Operating Procedure (SOP) in my life, and that is not to accept *any* roadblock. By

"First say to yourself what you would be; and then do what you have to do."

—EPICTETUS

planning ahead and having the goal clearly in my mind, I have been able to learn from failure and be confidently persistent in blasting through, over, under, or around any obstacle that stands between me and my goal. Please understand that I am speaking of intangible obstacles—not people. As I discussed in a previous chapter, maintaining good relationships is extremely important, and I do not mean to imply that I sacrifice relationships in order to achieve my goals. Quite the contrary, I make it a point to develop as many positive relationships as possible. What I am saying is that one of the most important principles I have learned is that I cannot be successful if I don't have a plan, and I cannot complete a good plan without setting goals and objectives.

THE PLANNING PROCESS

Significant accomplishments always begin with a vision or a dream.

As we work together to quicken achievement, I want to offer you what I have learned from more than twenty years of goal setting. To me, there are three major aspects of a good plan:

1. It is an action map that keeps me on track.

2. It is a tool that helps me measure my progress.

3. It is a reminder of why I decided to do what I am doing, and it actually helps keep me committed to the strategy.

A plan that does these things must include the following components:

A VISION FOR THE FUTURE. Significant accomplishments always begin with a vision or a dream. The ability to visualize future reality affords us a great deal of control over our success—or our lives, for that matter. Notice that I said a *great deal* of control, not *complete* control. There are always speed bumps in life. The difference for those who are really successful is often that they have a plan, a vision, and the focus that prevents a speed bump from becoming a roadblock. Plans begin with a clear vision for the future and are sustained by that vision when the going gets tough. Those who have some kind of a vision statement for their lives will always have something to come back to that will remind them of the purpose behind their goals.

AN OBJECTIVE ANALYSIS OF CURRENT CONDITIONS. Recognizing reality is always a good starting point for an effective plan. The importance of understanding our current situation gives us perspective about the action we need to take *from where we are right now.* This sounds simple, however, over the years I have found that many people

> *"The people who get on in this world are the people who get up and look for the circumstances they want, and, if they can't find them, make them."*
>
> —GEORGE BERNARD SHAW

with whom I have worked have skipped this feature, and it is a very important element of a good plan. The following example will make this principle clear.

Let's say you are awakened out of a sound sleep in the middle of the night, kidnapped, and immediately blindfolded. The kidnapper then inserts plugs in your ears so you can't hear anything. He loads you into the trunk of his car and drives for about an hour, making several left and right turns. Suddenly, he stops the car and dumps you out on the ground and quickly drives off. You remove the blindfold and the earplugs, but all you can see are trees, and there are no familiar landmarks. You look around and realize you are in the middle of an unmarked crossroad. You have survived—you are free and unharmed—and you just want to get home, but you have no idea where you are or which way to go.

You know perfectly well where your house is. You know the street, the address, the neighborhood, and the city. You can see your house clearly in your mind, but you can't figure out how to get there because you don't have a clue about where you are at that moment. All you can see are trees and endless roads, and you don't have a visual starting point or know a place to begin.

Planning is much the same way. We may have a clear picture of where we want to go; but if we don't know where we are beginning, the direction we establish may be flawed. We must have an objective analysis of our current situation in order to begin any planning process.

A COMMITMENT TO SETTING GOALS. Show me someone who doesn't know where he wants to go, and I will show you someone who won't go very far. When we plan, we need a clear understanding of what we are trying to accomplish. Setting and putting in writing specific goals will make us accountable to ourselves and to others. When we go on record by setting goals, we are saying to ourselves and the world around us, "I am going to do this!" Many people don't set goals because they don't want to put their feet in concrete and run the risk of failure. But a plan without goals is not a plan. Remember, long-term success in life requires the consistent accomplishment of predetermined objectives, and that means that plans must include goals.

A PLAN FOR ACCOMPLISHING THOSE GOALS. We need to know what we have to do to accomplish each goal we establish. Spending time working through the details of how we will get to where we want to go is well worth the effort, and it is a great way to build success into the plan. There are four keys to determining what must be done to accomplish our goals.

> *"What you get by achieving your goals is not as important as what you become by achieving your goals."*
>
> —ZIG ZIGLAR

1. *Specific Action Steps.* Every goal we establish will require specific actions. Identifying the action steps in the planning process does several things. First, it

requires us to think through the entire process. Second, it gives us a road map to follow that will keep us on track until the goal is accomplished. Third, because it involves linking action steps together in sequence, it helps us see that the goal is realistic (based on our values) and can be accomplished. At this point, we know we can do it, because the action steps are reasonable and possible.

2. *Established Timelines.* Established, specific timelines for reaching our goals help combat the human tendency to procrastinate. Whether we want to admit it or not, we all do procrastinate; and it is a destructive habit that we must learn to overcome. Timelines raise the bar of accountability (automated discipline, if you will).

> *"By losing your goal, you have lost your way."*
>
> —FRIEDRICH NIETZSCHE

Most of us have a "to do" list of some kind or another from which we work each day. The most critical items on our lists often have due dates attached to them. Then there are some items at the bottom of the lists that hang around longer than they should, usually because we have not decided they are important enough to be assigned a deadline. As a result, we put off doing them until we have more time. The problem is, it is hard to find the time for something when there is no fixed deadline for its completion. If we really want to accomplish our goals, we must establish timelines for completion of each overall goal, as well as each action step.

3. *Measured Success.* Another component of a good plan is some kind of evidence that proves that each goal has been met. For example, let's say a goal has been established to improve our company's competitive position through more effective use of the Internet. To accomplish that goal, we establish action steps to buy the necessary equipment, install the necessary software, train our people, establish a Web site, etc.

How can we measure success after we have completed all of the action steps? We need to develop measuring statements that describe what will happen as a result of accomplishing the goal. They may look something like these statements written for a business' goal to establish a Web site and implement new office technology:

1. All of our employees will have access to e-mail and will use it daily to communicate with each other and with our customers.

2. Our Internet Web site will be functional, and we will be receiving positive feedback from customers and prospective customers.

3. Our employees will have integrated Internet resources into their daily tasks, and their individual productivity will have improved significantly.

Critical Success Factors (CSFs) are another good tool for measuring success. They are factors that have been identified at the beginning of your plan that can help measure your results. I have Critical Success Factors in my goals program that I review every week to help me assess the status of my plan. Creating measuring statements and Critical Success Factors makes it easier to recognize success when it has been achieved. These statements can supplement statistics as a means for measuring success.

4. *Tools and Resources.* When a carpenter plans to build something, obviously the first step is deciding what will be needed to build it. How much lumber will be needed? What tools will be necessary? Is there a special item that may be hard to obtain? Anyone who has ever assembled anything understands how frustrating it can be to reach a critical point in the assembly process and not have the proper tools or materials to complete the task. The same principle applies in the planning process.

THE PEOPLE FACTOR

"A mind, once stretched by a new idea, never regains its original dimensions."

—OLIVER
WENDELL HOLMES

Goal setting is very important, and so is planning, but there is a third element in goal setting that many fail to recognize. One of the most important things I have learned is that I need help from other people if I want to consistently accomplish my goals. Often, other people have been the most important resource I have had in reaching the many goals I have set over the years.

Aside from the obvious conclusion that "more hands move more sand," people provide two unique tools that are vital to goal achievement: experience and synergy. As a case in point, I have long had the significant goal of authoring forty books. Until I was sitting in Sunday School one day a few years ago, I had no idea how to really achieve that goal. My previous stabs at writing and publishing books were less than successful, to put it mildly. I had been tempted to postpone the goal. But every quarter as I reviewed my life goals, I recognized my continued desire and, in spite of a lack of success, I kept it on the list.

Aside from the obvious conclusion that "more hands move more sand," people provide two unique tools that are vital to goal achievement: experience and synergy.

My goals are always fresh on my mind, and when the former sales executive of a major publishing company approached me at church to ask me about my consulting services, I quickly put two and two together. My organization helped him with his need, and he brought to me a wealth of publishing experience and know-how. He understood the dynamics of having the right cover design and layout. He knew how distributors, wholesalers, and bookstores worked together. And he knew the people who could help make all the right things happen for me.

Now, less than five years later, I am approaching the mid-point of my original goal of authoring forty books. This experience has further convinced me that no matter how much we may want to achieve something, we can't do it alone! Every person walking on this planet has a unique set of gifts and abilities that can challenge, motivate, and catapult us to a new level of thinking and achievement. By clearly knowing our goals and maintaining positive relationships, we can be ready when a goal is developed and we need help to achieve it.

Many people have a long list of former goals they never achieved. I suspect some of these unrealized goals were the result of not including other people. Sadly, many suffer from the "Lone Ranger Syndrome" (LRS): thinking they have to do it all by themselves to be considered truly successful.

While developing the concept for this book, I spoke with several professionals and solicited their opinions on some key issues. One of the questions we addressed was whether or not *everyone* needs help from others to be successful. Many people believed that there are some individuals who don't need the help of others, and they cited examples of inventors and artists who work alone in their laboratories and studios to create great new works. These responses caused me to do some serious thinking about how people create new things. *Do we really need the help of others to be successful?*

I came to the conclusion that many improvements and what we call "progress" begin in the form of ideas. Without ideas we would live in a perpetual status quo. It is intriguing to try to determine where ideas come from. How do they form in our minds? How are they shaped?

What stimulates our brains to think and ponder mysteries and questions that are vexing and curious?

How many original ideas have you had during the past six months? In your lifetime? I would suggest that you have had none— and neither have I. I simply believe no human being has ever had a completely *original* idea.

"Ideas are the root of creation."

—ERNEST DIMNET

Just in case you think I have taken leave of my senses and wonder if I have never used a telephone, never turned on an electric light, never traveled in an airplane, or never heard of nylon, plastic, fiber optics, computers, or fax machines, please allow me to explain.

I believe that none of the wonderful things invented in our lifetime are the result of anyone's having an original idea in the purest sense. These inventions came about as a result of combining *old* ideas to produce something new—by making improvements and changes to concepts that previously existed and by connecting pieces of knowledge that were previously unconnected. New inventions may *appear* to be the result of an original idea, but the only thing original

We observe, reason, and connect seemingly unrelated facts and eventually reach new conclusions.

about them is their function. I believe the ideas that spawned these inventions were a series of old ideas, combined in new, creative ways.

All of us have come up with some ideas we thought were original. What we actually did was piece together preexisting information and repackage it into something "new." The human brain is a reasoning machine, not a creator of new data from scratch. The Bible even tells us, *There is nothing new under the sun. Is there a thing of which it is said, "See, this is new"? It has been already, in the ages before us* (Ecclesiastes 1:9-10 RSV). Our ideas and conclusions depend on ideas and information that existed previously. We observe, reason, and connect seemingly unrelated facts and eventually reach new conclusions.

Our *creativity* and *originality* of thought depend on how well we can improve on the old ideas of others. We don't have original ideas—we collate and reposition old ideas into new combinations. The new combinations may produce things that have a new, original function or purpose, but the ideas themselves are not original.

What does this have to do with other people helping us accomplish our goals? What I have learned is that while I may "come up with" some good ideas from time to time, other people have influenced my thoughts and will also help me improve on my ideas. This helps me accomplish things faster, which brings me to the subject of speed.

Success Acceleration is about *quickening* the art of personal achievement. That means we want to learn how to do the things that work faster. Speed is a major key to success, because things change rapidly in our modern world, and we must adapt to those changes. We need other people to help us.

SPEED

Our personal experience is very important, but if our progress in life is restricted to our making observations on our own, we are in for a long, slow process. Learning from others and gaining their assistance and support not only allows us to be more productive, it also means we can accomplish things *faster.* The speed at which we work and produce is a primary factor in how successful we will be in the marketplace.

I can demonstrate the importance of speed by using a crowded restaurant as an example. A restaurant is typically limited to a certain number of tables and certain dining hours. The greater the number of people who can be processed through that restaurant within the available dining hours, the greater the revenue (and, presumably, the greater the profitability) for the restaurant. If customers spend long periods of time waiting for their food because the kitchen crew is slow or the server is disorganized, it means there are others who will not be seated and may leave the restaurant because they do not want to wait. A slow kitchen crew and a disorganized server can have a direct negative impact on the restaurant's total revenues.

Speed is critical to success. There is a constant push in business for greater productivity and higher quality. Productivity and speed are partners, and I believe that speed is one of the most important keys to the success of my own business.

THE JEARY THEORY

I believe the important elements of success include goal setting, a good work ethic, and a positive attitude. These are basic skills that most successful people employ in their businesses and in their personal lives. Even though these qualities have always been cornerstones of success, the business world has now reached a point where it demands speed of accomplishment as well.

I believe one of the chief reasons my own organization is successful is because we often sell our services and products emphasizing both quality *and* speed. The faster we can process and complete the client's task, the happier our customers will be. I can't count the number of times a customer has called in a crisis and given us an assignment with a short fuse. We don't complain about short fuses! We view them as opportunities that will put us even further ahead of our competition.

Important elements of success include goal setting, a good work ethic, and a positive attitude.

PRODUCTION BEFORE PERFECTION

I discovered this concept a little more than ten years ago, and it has literally revolutionized my life and my businesses. The basic premise is that procrastination is thrown out the window by simply taking action *now*. Even if the product is not perfect, that is okay. Obviously, brain surgery should be exempt from this idea, but in many cases the need for perfection is not as high as the benefits gained by getting the job done now. Occasionally there is indeed a requirement for delivering virtual perfection. Often in these cases we employ the "production before perfection" concept to generate a preliminary draft or sample to get confirmation on our direction, which leaves us in a position to incorporate changes. At that point we can put all hands on deck to produce a "perfect" product. Because this has been such a revolutionary concept in my life, I have devoted an entire chapter of this book to production before perfection where we will discuss this concept in greater detail.

"You may delay, but time will not."

—BENJAMIN FRANKLIN

Another thing we do in my business is regularly communicate with our customers and ask them why they like to do business with us. We want to know if we are maintaining our competitive position in their eyes and what we can do better and faster to get even more business. Our customers consistently say they give us contracts and projects because they know the work will be done quickly and meet the deadline for completion. They know my team will do whatever has to be done to complete a project as promised and will even deliver it ahead of schedule if possible.

I will admit that our work environment can be quite hectic when we have a critical job to do with little time to do it, but my people understand the importance of speed and are willing to do what it takes to meet deadlines and customer expectations. I have built many companies on speed, and the ability to deliver has won repeat business time and again. Speedy completion of work provides the opportunity to do more work, and more work means higher revenues, greater productivity, and higher profits. All this translates into a win/win situation.

> *"Lost wealth may be replaced by industry, lost knowledge by study, lost health by temperance or medicine, but lost time is gone forever."*
>
> —SAMUEL SMILES

There is no way my organization could accomplish what it does without the help of many people. My theory is that I should treat them all as if they were visitors who just stepped into my life with a ton of information that will help me be more successful. I can be creative and come up with "new" ideas only when I am exposed to the experience and ideas of other people. Then I can make connections from my own experience and come up with better ways to work and better ways to win. This is the *Jeary Theory:* I know I need the help of others, so I keep many informed about my goals and objectives. I want them to know what they can do to help me, in the same way I want to know their goals and how I can help them.

I regularly seek the opinions of all of my associates, and I use this information to improve and be more productive. I read and summarize books and magazines, listen to audiotapes on various topics related to my goals, and do just about anything else I need to do to keep a steady flow of new information coming into my life. The more relevant information I can process, the faster I can move and grow. That is the way it works. Accelerated success is all about speed and productivity, speed and competition, and speed and profitability.

VIPs

(VERY IMPORTANT POINTS)

    Significant accomplishments always begin with a vision or a dream.

    Spending time working through the details of how we will get to where we want to go is well worth the effort, and it is a great way to build success into the plan.

    Our creativity and originality of thought depend on how well we can improve on the old ideas of others.

    Speed is critical to success. For accelerated success, productivity and speed are partners.

    Many people suffer from the "Lone Ranger Syndrome" (LRS): thinking they have to do it all by themselves to be considered truly successful.

Section Three:

TACTICS

7

YOU CAN'T DO IT ALONE!

We have laid the foundation for accelerated success and defined three solid strategies to employ in the process. In the remaining chapters, we will be discussing specific tactics that I believe have been vital to the achievement of my goals and can do the same for you.

We have talked about the fact that success cannot be achieved without interacting with and gleaning ideas from other people. These two elements—people and skills—can be artfully blended together to accelerate achievement and increase effectiveness. I believe my "connection database" of acquaintances, friends, associates, and business contacts is the most valuable professional asset I possess.

If we never received any fresh, new ideas from others, our only options would be to keep doing the same things the same way we have always done them—and keep getting the same results!

PEOPLE NEED PEOPLE

If we never received any fresh, new ideas from others, our only options would be to keep doing the same things the same way we have always done them—and keep getting the same results! You are reading *Success Acceleration* to get new ideas, because you want different results, and you want to quicken your achievement.

If you can accept the premise that you are incapable of originating ideas by yourself, it will help you see how critical your need for assistance from others really is.

MAROONED ON AN ISLAND

To illustrate the point of how people think, create, and accomplish things, let's imagine the following scenario. For the sake of this discussion, imagine that you were marooned on an uninhabited island as an infant and somehow survived and grew up without the help of other humans. Imagine the island as being rather small, with only a beach, several varieties of trees, a pool of fresh water, and a cave. There is no animal life on the island. You have never seen a book, a television, a telephone, or another human being. As far as you know, the entire world consists of just you, the beach, the trees, the pool, and the cave. There is nothing more.

"The world hates change, yet it is the only thing that has brought progress."

—CHARLES F. KETTERING

After a few years on the island, you have observed and assimilated all you can about the island. There is little else to learn, and your creative potential is limited to what you know about those few things on the island. You are the most unconsciously incompetent human on the planet! You don't have a clue about what you don't know, yet you probably believe you know everything there is to know. Without new things or other people to stimulate your mind and your thinking, you are doomed to a life of non-change and repetitious behavior—doing the same things over and over again, every day.

FORMING NEW IDEAS

Often, when we run out of old ideas upon which we can improve, we create "new" ideas (new to us) by conducting experiments. Experiments involve a line of reasoning that says, "I wonder what would happen if I do this, or that." Human experimentation is the wild card of creativity.

In our example of the deserted island, let's examine how experimentation might help you advance your knowledge. Let's say that one day you see lightning strike a tree and cause the tree to burst into flames. You also notice the flames are hot; and, because the night is chilly, you like the way the fire

> "Progress is impossible without change, and those who cannot change their minds cannot change anything."
>
> —GEORGE BERNARD SHAW

makes you feel warm. Your most reasonable hope for future warmth is another lightning strike that will start another fire. You may not even think about trying to start a fire on your own.

Then one day you are hanging out in the cave, killing time by pitching some flat stones against the cave wall. Suddenly, you pitch a stone, and it produces a spark when it strikes another stone at the base of the wall. You are reminded of the lightning that struck the tree and created the fire, and you have a flash that it might be possible to create a fire without lightning. At this point, you have made a connection, part of which is based on old information and past observation (the effect of lightning), and part of which is based on the result of an accidental event (the creation of a spark by the striking of two stones). From the connection you make between lightning and the spark, you develop a theory about how you might be able to build a fire. But you still don't have enough information to turn the idea into reality, so you begin to experiment.

Your experiment begins by attempting to recreate the spark you produced by accident. You have been pitching stones in your cave for a long time, so you wonder why this spark suddenly occurred. It has never happened before. You examine the stones. One by one you pick them up and strike them together. Nothing happens. You are baffled and perplexed. Then, you get the idea that maybe the stones are different and that striking them together in different combinations might produce a spark. You then begin a systematic experiment of striking all the stones together in every possible combination. After endless hours of striking stones together with no result, you finally strike two stones together, and a spark is created. You repeat the strike, and another spark flies off the face of the stones. You compare these two stones and notice that they are different in appearance from the other stones. You don't realize it, but you have discovered flint!

Many additional experiments will be necessary before you can repeatedly harness the sparks from the flint and produce a fire, but the process is underway, and you have a chance of creating something new—fire. The fire itself will not be new, but the ability to create fire will be revolutionary to you. It may even be the source of a lifetime of new discoveries. For your purposes, however, you need to recognize that all of this creativity was founded on the knowledge you gained through observation and experimentation.

Nowhere in the process did you concoct an idea that wasn't somehow linked to your past experience or your experiments.

Nowhere in the process did you concoct an idea that wasn't somehow linked to your past experience or your experiments. Your mind could not conceive of the existence of fire until you saw it produced by the lightning. Your mind could not conceive of building a fire yourself until the accidental event of the sparking stones. Through this entire process, you did not have one original thought. You simply made some connections and conducted some experiments in response to your observations.

Let's speculate that one day you are sitting quietly by your newly made fire, and you notice something in the ocean that is being propelled toward the beach by the waves. As the object gets closer, it becomes recognizable. It's another person! With a bit of fear and trepidation, you run down to the shore and wait for the surf to deliver this poor soul onto the beach.

You take your new friend to your comfortable fire to get him warm. You smugly anticipate how amazed he will be when you demonstrate your "original" invention (fire). However, when your new friend sees the fire, he doesn't appear to be too impressed. You are stunned by your guest's lack of amazement and disappointed that he doesn't question how you created such an incredible phenomenon. You had spent years developing the final product after discovering the sparking stones, and you want to tell this person how hard you worked to perfect this miracle. The apathy of your visitor about your fire making is puzzling.

> "Every really new idea looks crazy at first."
>
> —ALFRED NORTH WHITEHEAD

After your guest has warmed up and the two of you have become more comfortable with each other, you ask him if he is curious about how you managed to create this wonderful fire. The visitor looks at you and says, "No . . . I presumed you used a match." The ensuing hours of conversation produce a great sense of humility as you learn about matches and many other things. As the evening progresses, your visitor tells you about airplanes, telephones, computers, and other things you can hardly imagine. As your visitor shares his knowledge, your little fire seems puny by comparison.

As days go by and you learn more from your island visitor, it becomes clear that this person can have a profound effect on your existence and the way you live. You think about the time you invested in learning to build your fire, and you realize how much sooner you would have been enjoying fire if your new friend had washed up on the beach years earlier. You are struck by the impact your visitor could have had on your life by sharing his knowledge and experience with you earlier.

Your visitor quickly helps you understand that there is more to the world than your island and that both of you would benefit by leaving the island. You learn that traveling to other places would be possible if you built a boat. Absorbing the knowledge of your friend eventually transforms your entire existence and puts you in a position to live in ways you could not have imagined on your own.

WHAT'S THE MESSAGE?

Even though while you were on the island you learned to make fire by yourself, the purpose of this story is to further illustrate that none of us has truly original thoughts. We make observations, we experiment, and we combine our observations and experiments into the discovery of "new" things.

Learning from others and gaining their help and support not only means we can be more fruitful and productive, it also means we can accomplish things faster.

I believe one of the most valuable illustrations from this story is how creativity actually works and how new discoveries are made. We must understand that we are dependent on the acquisition of information to spur our reasoning processes and stimulate our creative juices. This story demonstrates that information we need most often comes from at least one of two sources: observations based on our experience, or contact with other people.

QUICKENING YOUR SUCCESS

Our personal experience is very important; but if our progress in life is restricted to our own observations, we are in for a long, slow, and faulty process. Learning from others and gaining their help and support not only means we can be more fruitful and productive, it also means we can accomplish things *faster.* The speed at which we work and produce is a primary factor in how competitive we are in the marketplace. Our competitive readiness directly affects our success and achievement.

There is another theory I want to present about the critical nature of new information and achievement. It is called "profound knowledge."

PROFOUND KNOWLEDGE

W. Edward Deming, the American who helped the Japanese rebuild their economy after World War II and one of the pioneers of what became known as Total Quality Management (TQM), believed that profound knowledge was a *system* every business and organization should adopt to insure its long-term success. Deming defined profound knowledge as "information invited from the outside and imported into an organization." In other words, an organization with this system would systematically invite new information into the business to produce change and improvement. The same principle applies to us individually.

Without a periodic infusion of new information, businesses can become stagnant as they continually recycle the same ideas of the same people, over and over again.

Few professionals dispute the idea that businesses and organizations must be willing to endure constant change to remain competitive. Better ways of creating, marketing, and delivering products are critical to growth and long-term success. The ideas of people who work in a business are one source of change and improvement. Unfortunately, without a periodic infusion of new information, businesses can become stagnant as they continually recycle the same ideas of the same people, over and over again. In theory, the employees of that business "island" would eventually learn all they could from each other, and the business culture would become a bureaucratic system of people doing the same things but somehow hoping for better results.

For new information to be truly new, it must come from an external source. Picture the island in our previous example, and remember the day the new visitor was washed up on the beach. Prior to his arrival, you had functioned in a closed information system. Change and improvement were slow to develop. The visitor came from places that were different and very advanced, and he introduced ideas that revolutionized your world.

New information imported from the outside has the power to break through people's *unconscious incompetence* (not knowing what they don't know) and elevate them to a state of *conscious incompetence* (knowing they don't know). When people know they don't know, they are then able to move forward and learn new things that will create change and improvement.

Every teacher was once a student. Every master artist was influenced by the work and technique of other artists as he developed his own talent and style.

NEW INFORMATION FUELS THE SUCCESS ENGINE

I hope you are convinced that none of us has original ideas in the purest sense. We are ingenious observers gifted with powerful abilities to reason and create "new" things from old ideas. Even the great master artists of the past who worked alone with their wonderful creations had a need for new information. Every teacher was once a student. Every master artist was influenced by the work and technique of other artists as he developed his own talent and style. People who are deprived of new information change little about themselves. Those who don't change have difficulty improving, and those who can't improve will struggle to achieve and maintain success.

Remember that a requirement for the system of profound knowledge is that the new information must be invited. People have a way of resisting anything they believe is being given them against their will. No one wants to be forced to change, just as no one enjoys being forced to sit through "learning experiences" he doesn't believe he needs. However, if we hope to quicken our success, we must be committed to inviting the assistance of others. It is a mind-set that willingly acknowledges that we need help. The question should always be, "Who can best help me accomplish this objective?"

> *"It is one of the most beautiful compensations of life, that no man can sincerely try to help another without helping himself."*
>
> —RALPH WALDO EMERSON

GO FOR IT

Understanding this concept of how creativity and change really work revolutionized my approach to personal achievement and the way I work with other people. As the leader of my organization, my job is to keep people informed and ensure that we have a steady inflow of new information to keep us sharp and competitive. I accomplish this task by employing the strategy of continually sharing information with everyone. This strategy involves recognizing that I need other people to help me be successful. Without others I am alone on an isolated island, with little hope for improvement or change—and that is synonymous with losing.

CREATING YOUR "CONNECTION DATABASE"

Hopefully, you are now convinced you need the help of others to quicken your achievement. If so, it may be helpful to create your own "connection database." As I mentioned previously, I have been creating mine for almost two decades, and I will continue building it as long as I live. The key to this effort is a primary mind-set that involves being aware of others who may be able to work with me over a long period of time. If I think I may be able to help them or they may be able to help me in the future, I add them to my list of contacts.

Without others I am alone on an isolated island, with little hope for improvement or change—and that is synony-mous with losing.

The first step in identifying people to add to your database is to meet a lot of people and learn as much about them as possible. This involves really listening to what others have to say and asking a lot of questions. Even though this may be awkward for some, overcoming any hesitancy to meet and visit with strangers is a part of the mind-set that must be developed.

I am constantly on the alert for people with whom I can build a relationship. I learned a long time ago that you never know how the person you meet today might be able to work with you in the future. I travel a lot and spend a lot of time in airplanes and airports, but I very seldom spend that time alone with my thoughts. I am always aware of the people around me, and I make mental notes about what they are doing, reading, or saying. I make a point of introducing myself

> *"The most important single ingredient in the formula of success is knowing how to get along with people."*
>
> —THEODORE ROOSEVELT

and asking them questions about what they do. I learn as much as I can about them personally and professionally. I particularly want to know about any unique skills they may possess that might be helpful in the future. I also want to know if they might need assistance from me. This is the way I have found some of the most valuable people in my "connection database."

In 1995 I was flying to Detroit, Michigan, to do some work for Chrysler Corporation, my largest client at that time. Across the aisle from my seat were two gentlemen traveling together, and I certainly recognized one of them. He was Zig Ziglar, one of the foremost experts in the world on success and motivation. I introduced myself to Zig and his traveling companion, and we ended up having a lively conversation all the way to Detroit. The man sitting next to Zig was Jim Norman, who was the president and CEO of Zig's company. While I was incredibly happy to meet Zig, I was fascinated with the man who was with him. I was thinking, *What kind of skills are required for a person to be Zig Ziglar's key man, and how could a person like this help me?*

To make a long story short, Jim Norman has become one of my best friends and one of my most valuable resources during the past five years. Jim left The Ziglar Corporation in 1996 and returned to independent consulting work. He has provided priceless assistance to me as I have transitioned my organization into higher productivity and growth. My relationship with Jim would never have happened if I had failed to introduce myself on that flight to Detroit.

In addition to my relationship with Jim, I was also able to develop a relationship with Zig Ziglar himself. Zig's company embraced my *Inspire Any Audience* training program as their primary curriculum for training presentation skills. Zig has endorsed my books and has helped me in many other ways. My relationship with Zig and Jim has opened doors for me with many other people as well. All of this was the result of one conversation on an airplane.

I shared the story of meeting Zig and Jim because you probably recognize Zig's name. I can tell you that the same scenario has happened hundreds of times with other people—some you may know, but most you would not. Many of these people have been incredible resources for me. Some have become close friends, some have become long-standing clients, and some have coauthored books with me. I am always looking for people to meet and am anxious to learn about them, because you never know where a short conversation may lead. It is a mind-set I have developed over the years. Everyone I meet is a candidate for inclusion in my "connection database." They are all like strangers who have washed up on my beach, loaded with information and ideas that I need and can use to quicken my achievement.

I need to point out here that help is not a one-way street. I learned a long time ago that people are willing to help me because I always figure out ways to help them *first!* Every time I meet a new person, I think, *What can I do for them?* Zig Ziglar's famous quote, "You can have everything in life you want if you just help enough other people get what they want," is the driving principle behind my development of relationships.

> "Always be nice to people on the way up; because you'll meet the same people on the way down."
>
> —WILSON MIZNER

When I first meet people, I also try to find out what I have in common with them. The more I know about them, the better our relationship will be. My primary creed for success is to give value and do more than is expected. I do my best to live by this principle and practice it in all that I do. I sincerely want to help others, and I look for ways to help *them* be more successful. I want to know their goals and dreams, and I want them to know mine. If I can do something that will help them, I do it. I listen to them. I learn about their lives, and I rejoice with them in their success. And, in the process, my success is accelerated beyond my own abilities.

⚑

VIPs
(VERY IMPORTANT POINTS)

⚑ We must understand that we are dependent on others for the information to spur our reasoning processes and stimulate our creative juices.

⚑ Those who don't change have difficulty improving, and those who can't improve will struggle to achieve and maintain success.

⚑ Learning from others and gaining their help and support not only means we can be more fruitful and productive, it also means we can accomplish things *faster*.

⚑ If we hope to quicken our success, we must be committed to inviting the assistance of others.

LEARN FROM THE WINNERS

One of my favorite tactics for quickening success is the study of something I call "Modeling Distinctions." Distinctions, obviously, are those things that make people stand apart from others, such as a unique voice or mannerism. The distinctions I study, however, go far beyond that. I am interested in the distinctions that have made other people successful so that I can model them.

As I have continued to develop relationships over the years, I have spent a lot of time studying the distinctions of the various people I have met. The power of those distinctions emerges when I apply them in a process called "benchmarking." Simply put, when a company's leadership wants to improve its business in a certain area, management often seeks another company that has already achieved the desired results and then studies what it did to accomplish them. Major corporations frequently spend large amounts of money to gain the knowledge they seek and sometimes actually send out teams of their own employees to visit companies being studied. These teams often create models for their own companies to copy based on the distinctions they have observed,

*Listen to advice and
accept instruction,
that you may
gain wisdom for
the future.*

—PROVERBS
19:20 RSV

and the result is a quickening of their organizations' ability to achieve their desired goals.

Let me explain here that "benchmarks" and "benchmarking" are not the same. Benchmarks are used to measure performance and progress. When an employee is undergoing an annual review, for example, benchmarks may be established to determine whether the person is meeting his or her performance goals. Benchmarking, on the other hand, is generally described as an activity designed to discover and attain an understanding of the best specific practices responsible for outstanding achievement.

You can imagine how the benchmarking process can accelerate a company's ability to achieve. Modeling (or benchmarking) often allows a company to avoid mistakes that are made in experimentation and discovery and to concentrate on proven methods and techniques used by the modeled firm(s). Another benefit is that skeptics within an organization are often convinced through this process to adopt certain practices *after* they have witnessed the success those practices produced in the benchmarked company.

This process is an effective and popular business concept, and it is also a powerful concept for individuals to use in the same way. If you want to change the principles in your belief window in a hurry, and thus accelerate your overall success, I challenge you to model the distinctions of people who have been successful and who have track records as high achievers.

Let me give you a good example. I was hired some years ago by the Chrysler Corporation to go behind the scenes at the Ritz Carlton Hotel chain and find out what made them so successful. By benchmarking, I was able to find out how they give such exceptional service. One factor is that they have their processes and procedures down to an exact science. They have signage *everywhere*—where to place each pallet that is delivered, where to put specific foods, where to store each type of linen, etc. They have, in effect, shortened the training curve so successfully that it has empowered their employees to focus almost entirely on service. The results have been phenomenal.

Benchmarking the Ritz Carlton was an amazing experience. The bottom line was that it led Chrysler to think "outside the box" and produce new ideas. Chrysler was able, for example, to internalize some of the Ritz Carlton's customer satisfaction principles and apply them to the automobile industry—which resulted in higher customer satisfaction ratings from Chrysler customers. The best practices of the hotel had many universal applications for other types of businesses seeking to improve customer satisfaction.

"If there is any one secret of success, it lies in the ability to get the other person's point of view and see things from that person's angle as well as from your own."

—HENRY FORD

Besides identifying *new* "best practices" for a company, benchmarking also allows an organization to examine its *existing* practices and compare them with those of the benchmarked firm. This process alone can produce improvement and higher levels of achievement. Benchmarking is designed to import new knowledge into a business for the purpose of facilitating change. Receiving information from benchmarking is equivalent to a stranger's being washed up on the island beach full of profound knowledge—it can change an organization forever.

BENCHMARKING PEOPLE

Benchmarking successful people requires a mindset of constant observation and study, and one that is centered on others.

In the same way that businesses benchmark other organizations to determine their best practices, we can benchmark successful people to see what has worked for them. I have been doing this for years. I learned many years ago that other people have already done what I want to do, and by benchmarking their success and modeling their unique distinctions, I have been able to accelerate my own achievement.

There is one slight difference, however, between benchmarking businesses and modeling the distinctions of other people. Benchmarking successful people requires a mindset of constant observation and study, and one that is centered on others.

Since many people tend to be "self-centered" and not consciously observant, this may require a fundamental change in our behavior.

Although other people may model the distinctions of others, I have met few who take it to the extent that I do. This is one of the most valuable skills I have developed. My process is very systematic and comprehensive. The first thing I had to develop to properly model the distinctions of others is called "sensory acuity." Simply put, this is the practice of constantly looking, listening, smelling, hearing—using those four senses to take in what is going on around me, no matter where I am. This creates the mental environment that helps me identify people who know things I need to know.

I am looking for people who know something I don't know. I find them everywhere. I see them on television (I am a big fan of A&E's *Biography* program), I read about them in books, and I meet them everywhere I go. As I try to always be aware of my surroundings, I work to keep my sensory acuity in the "on" position to help me spot the opportunities to observe people who have special and unique characteristics.

Using sensory acuity is like wearing a special pair of glasses that highlight the distinctions of others. These glasses help me see the little things successful people do. (They also help me notice the little things that unsuccessful people do, which can be equally valuable in most cases.) I observe and study the way successful people think and act. I study the way they dress. I observe the types of equipment they buy and carry with them. I observe the tools they use for taking notes in meetings. I observe the way they conduct themselves in meetings. I look for patterns in the way they do things. I look for processes as well. I also look for the things that set them apart from others and directly contribute to their success.

When I meet a person who exudes confidence and has the persona of achievement, my sensory acuity kicks in and I make a point of getting to know more about that individual. However, I may also study someone I have never heard of before if that person has a technique or skill that I need to learn. In that case, obviously, either I have to find someone else who knows about that person, or I have to find a book or other objective source that will tell me what I need to know. This is usually the way I approach learning about highly successful celebrities or famous people who have lived before me.

> "Knowledge is of two kinds. We know a subject ourselves, or we know where we can find information on it."
>
> —SAMUEL JOHNSON

A good example of someone I have benchmarked from the past is Thomas Edison, the great inventor. Edison was an incredibly productive person; the sheer number of things in which he was involved during his lifetime is staggering. How did Edison become so productive? How did he find the time to do all that he did? I learned that one of Edison's distinctions was that he did not work traditional hours. Neither did he sleep the way most people sleep. Edison took short naps and worked at different times around the clock.

I don't recommend living exactly the way Edison lived, because it is not conducive to a well-rounded family life. Most of our spouses and families would likely object to Edison's lifestyle. However, the distinction Edison has shown me is that I can be more productive if I do not have fixed working hours. I don't start working just because it is 8:00 A.M. or quit working because it is 5:00 P.M. I have created a working environment that will allow me to do what I need to do when I have the time to do it. If I wake up at 3:00 A.M. and know that I probably won't be able to go back to sleep, I get up and do something. My friends, business associates, and clients are never surprised to receive faxes or e-mail from me at all hours of the day or night.

The answer to every challenge you may have can probably be found in the life of some person, somewhere, who has overcome that same challenge.

I encourage you to learn as much as you can from people you have never known. If you have a problem being productive, model the distinctions of someone like Edison who was incredibly productive. If you have trouble being creative, find someone who was creative and learn about him or her. If you have trouble being organized, find a person who knows about organization and model that person's distinctions. The answer to every challenge you may have can probably be found in the life of some person, somewhere, who has overcome that same challenge.

I am sure you have heard of Lee Iacocca, the former Chairman of Chrysler Corporation who led the transformation of the company from failure to success. Although I have done a considerable amount of consulting and training for Chrysler, I have never had the opportunity to meet Mr. Iacocca, who retired in 1991. Did that stop me from modeling his distinctions? Absolutely not. I have worked with many other people who did know Mr. Iacocca—some of whom knew him quite well. The people included his personal bodyguard, his executive assistant, and the president of Chrysler. Through them, I was able to model some of Mr. Iacocca's distinctions. Also, I have read and studied the books that have been published about him, and I have found them to be very helpful.

> *"Minds are like parachutes. They only function when they are open."*
>
> —SIR JAMES DEWAR

Another valuable way I model distinctions is to hire people with specific talents to help me with certain projects and tasks. Though I keep my core staff very small, I have access to and use scores of other people on an "as needed" basis. When I work with these special people, I make a point to observe everything they do and the way they do it. Even if I think it is something I am already doing well, I still observe and ask questions, because I want to constantly polish and add to my distinctions. I am always looking for improvement.

I have also developed another modeling system that involves the way I process information from the books I read. Every year I read and/or study at least 100 books in order to glean the best practices and distinctions from each book. Then I summarize and recap each book in one or two pages from the points I have highlighted into a format that allows me to use the information in a variety of ways. One of the main ways I use the recaps is to share them with friends, associates, and clients so they can benefit from the information. After reviewing a recap, they may decide to read the book in its entirety or simply reference the core concepts over and over.

Meeting people and building long-term relationships with them gives me the most frequent opportunities to learn. When I have the opportunity to talk with successful people, I make it a point to continually tap their knowledge during our conversations. I am constantly looking for opportunities to benchmark and model—when I play golf, in social settings, on an airplane, in church, etc. I want to know how people think. I want to know how they handle situations that I find difficult. I want to obtain their input about the things I am doing so I can do them better. I am always searching for principles that will help me make better decisions.

There are many special people in my life who have provided excellent models for me in critical areas. One such person who has been a very important influence on my life has been my father-in-law. He has shown me what it means to be a great father. He raised two marvelous daughters. No matter when they needed his help, he would drop whatever he was doing and give them his undivided attention. I have learned much about being a father by watching him, and I have also learned from others who know him. I have asked many of these people to share their memories about how he raised his children, and it has made a tremendous impact on my life.

I also have benefited often from relationships with people who are ten to twenty years my senior. They have experienced decades of life and are valuable resources to benchmark. In talking with them, I have realized they have shared some distinctions that I should *not* model— things they feel they could have done better, such as spending more time with their children instead of working so many hours to accumulate wealth. I respect their experience and am open to listen to what they are saying.

Other people have already done what you want to do. You, too, can accelerate your achievement by benchmarking their successes and modeling their distinctions.

VIPs
(VERY IMPORTANT POINTS)

⚑   Benchmarking is an activity designed to discover and attain an understanding of the best specific practices responsible for outstanding achievement.

⚑   Benchmarking successful people requires a mind-set of constant observation and study, and one that is centered on others.

⚑   The answer to every challenge you may have can probably be found in the life of some person, somewhere, who has overcome that same challenge.

⚑   If you want to change the principles in your belief window in a hurry, and thus accelerate your overall success, model the distinctions of people who have been successful.

9

THE POWER OF YOUR PRESENTATION

For the past decade, I have enjoyed a flourishing career of teaching and coaching successful people in the art of effective presentations. This has been my passion, because I firmly believe that the people who become most successful are those who are able to skillfully convince and persuade other people.

Presentations are much more than "public speaking" opportunities. We make presentations any time we attempt to get agreement from another person. My own interest in improving presentation skills began in the public speaking arena, but I discovered the powerful application of presentation skills in the business arena through my own experience. How I began my quest to improve this area of my business life is an interesting story, even though I can't say it was much fun at the time.

The people who become most successful are those who are able to skillfully convince and persuade other people to take action on their behalf.

In the late 1980s I spent some time as a national speaker for American Business Seminars (ABS), and it was a rude awakening for me. I traveled to a new city every week and delivered a presentation to a captive audience. After each presentation, my promoter would escort me up to a hotel room and tell me what I did wrong. He would assail me with a long list of my mistakes, and the weekly assaults convinced me I needed to improve. My promoter knew it, and my audiences knew it! It was often embarrassing and definitely a humbling experience. I vividly remember standing in front of a room and witnessing detachment on the faces of the poor souls who had chosen to come there to hear me talk. I saw firsthand my inability to produce much positive action from my listeners. It was obvious that I had a lot to learn and that I would have to study and work hard to acquire skills that would inform, entertain, and inspire audiences to action.

My experience with ABS was one of those life-changing events that are often only fully appreciated years down the line. Since that time, my life has become an ongoing quest to acquire and develop my own presentation skills, but also to help others improve their skills. It has been a rewarding journey thus far. When I wrote my first book, *Inspire Any Audience*, I believed the most significant thing I could write would be an "ultimate presenter's handbook" because of the importance of presentation skills, both public and personal, in a person's success.

> *"One of the best ways to persuade others is with your ears—by listening to them."*
>
> —DEAN RUSK

I have met many people who don't have an appreciation for the powerful relationship between presentation skills and success. Frequently, I have encountered opinions that presentation skills are important and probably should be improved, but only after "more important" skills are refined. I can hardly criticize anyone who takes this approach, since my own attitude was similar prior to my experience with ABS. My embarrassment and ineffectiveness as a presenter were a direct result of my not taking this subject seriously. I did not have the presentation skills I needed to be a successful speaker and, even worse, I had not made obtaining those skills a high priority in my own quest for success.

I believe mastering the ability to effectively communicate and present ideas is the most difficult challenge but also the most rewarding strategy available to anyone involved with other people. Dale Carnegie wrote that 85 percent of a person's financial success is related to his or her personality and ability to lead people. I completely concur with this assessment.

COMMUNICATE EFFECTIVELY

A vital principle I have learned is this: *When everything else is equal, the ability to effectively present and communicate ideas is the greatest single factor in success!* I know that my own success has frequently depended on my ability to motivate others to take positive action on my behalf and, more often than not, it was not a public audience I was trying to convince. Communication and presentation are the key tools I use to enlist the help and support of other people.

The following example tragically illustrates the point that strong communication and presentation skills can be the determining factor in winning or losing when everything else is equal.

When everything else is equal, the ability to effectively present and communicate ideas is the greatest single factor in success!

There was a football coach who had all of the gifts and abilities necessary to be a great success. As a collegiate coach, he won 85 percent of the games he coached. In fact, he had the highest winning percentage of any college coach in the history of college football. He appeared in post-season bowl games virtually every year that he coached a team, and his teams frequently won national championships. In his first three years as a professional football coach, he produced three division championships and one Super Bowl victory. He was an *outstanding* football coach, based solely on his winning record that spanned more than twenty-five years.

However, if you were to ask the average football fan what he or she thought of this person when he was coaching professional football, most of the responses would be less than favorable. When his team lost, fans and media alike viciously attacked him and called for his termination. When his team won, the criticism level dropped, but there was rarely any public praise for his role in the victory.

Why was the public perception of this coach so negative? The public opinion was not really justified by his actual coaching record. It was driven by something else, and I believe it was his incredibly poor communication and presentation skills. I watched several of this coach's press conferences, and his performance was always very predictable.

1. He frequently had something in his mouth, which gave the effect that he was mumbling when he spoke.

2. He usually avoided eye contact with his audience; however, when he did look at the audience, his expression resembled a hostile glare.

3. He rarely smiled or attempted to transmit any feeling of warmth to his listeners.

4. He used profanity and other expletives throughout his presentation.

5. Everything he said seemed to have been delivered with little or no advance planning or preparation.

6. He gave the impression that he did not care what anyone thought about him, his team, or anything he had to say.

Is it any wonder that this coach managed to create a hornet's nest of negative opinion? While this example may be negative, it demonstrates the importance of presentation skills. I often wonder how much greater the coach's influence and career may have been if he had recognized the importance of developing good presentation skills. Would the public's perception have been different if he had developed a strategy to become an effective communicator? I somehow believe that he would have been openly recognized as one of the greatest coaches who ever lived! His actual coaching record supports that conclusion, but his woeful presentation skills prevented that from happening. This story dramatically demonstrates the critical influence presentation skills can have on success.

THE UNDISCOVERED SECRET OF SUCCESS

As vividly seen in the example above, communication and presentation skills are catalytic in nature and play a direct role in determining the results achieved. Few people actually understand this truth and incorporate into their plans and objectives the strategy of improving these skills. Consequently, I am convinced that the presentation skill is "the undiscovered secret of success."

Life is a series of presentations, and our success is dependent upon how we present ourselves on a daily basis.

I believe that life is a series of presentations, and our success is dependent upon how we present ourselves on a daily basis. In the same manner that we need effective communication and presentation skills to deliver a powerful presentation to a *public* audience, we must rely on those same skills when we interact privately with people on a daily basis—if we hope to achieve the same results. If we are to inspire others to help us be success-ful, we need to understand what motivates people to take action.

People act as a result of making a choice, and the choices they make eventually come down to one of two decisions: They will, or they won't! Those decisions are driven by (1) what they believe, (2) how they think, and (3) how they feel about things. Therefore, if I want someone to take positive action in my behalf, I have to do three things:

"Before speaking, consider the interpretation of your words as well as their intent."

—ANDREW ALDEN

1. I have to help the person believe what I am saying.
2. I have to relate to the way the person thinks.
3. I have to help the person feel good about helping me.

I want people to work with me because it is something they want to do. I also want them to benefit from whatever it is they are going to do in my behalf. I practice the philosophy of "win-win" in everything I do. As I share my goals and objectives with others, I make a point of explaining what I believe the "win" will be for both of us. People will take positive action when they are convinced there is a win-win situation, but we have to do the convincing. However, there is a difference between convincing and manipulating. When someone is convinced of something, he believes in it. When he has been manipulated into taking action, he doesn't necessarily believe in what he is doing. The distinction between working on "shared goals" is materially different from getting someone to do something he really doesn't want to do.

TRADITIONAL COMPONENTS OF SUCCESS

I believe most "success experts" will agree that four important components of success are: goal-setting, a strong work ethic, a positive attitude, and self-discipline/persistence. Each of these characteristics is crucial to the success process. The question is, when we consistently practice these four qualities, is there anything we can add to the mix to produce the winning edge we seek? I believe that gaining a winning edge involves how effectively we tell our story, present our case, or communicate our goals and objectives to others. Let's look at these four qualities and see how critical communication and presentation skills are to each.

Gaining a winning edge involves how effectively we tell our story, present our case, or communicate our goals and objectives to others.

Goal-setting. Goal-setting and planning are the two ingredients that are fundamental to a solid goals program. But for our purposes here, let's look at the planning part of the process. When we establish our goals and create our plans to accomplish those goals, we must think through the elements of the plan that will require assistance from others. There are few goals that do not involve other people in some way.

Most successful people recognize that goal-setting skills are important, but, amazingly, the importance of building a strong communication and presentation strategy is frequently overlooked. Many people have a long list of goals they have never achieved. Unfortunately, some of these unrealized goals were probably the result of not being able to communicate and present ideas effectively.

No progress is made on a goal until someone, somewhere, takes some action. Once we are assured that we have taken all the action required of us toward the achievement of a particular goal, it is then our responsibility to convince the other people involved to take action on our behalf. To do that, we must effectively communicate what we would like to happen. This means that what we say to them and how we say it is vital to our success. Obviously, communication and presentation skills are worthy of serious study if we want to accelerate the process.

Strong work ethic. The world is full of people waiting to win the lottery or hit it big at the racetrack, but the odds are that success will never be achieved by such methods. Such people have nothing of themselves invested in that kind of reward, and there is no sense of personal satisfaction. In every respect, nothing substitutes for hard work.

I believe my willingness to work hard has played a huge role in the success I have enjoyed. For many years, I traveled more than 200,000

147

miles each year, and I usually work ten to twelve hours virtually every business day. I am willing to invest whatever time it takes to get a job done and to produce the results my clients and customers expect. However, just because I am willing to work long and hard doesn't mean I will be efficient or effective. All of my hard work will be less fruitful if I am unable to effectively communicate and present my ideas and objectives to others.

I make a point of approaching every business conversation as if I am making a presentation. When I have an idea I want to share with someone or need something from another person to help me be more successful, how effectively I make my case and communicate my message determines whether I will be able to enlist their support in the form of positive action. Whether I am in my office or on an airplane, I am always ready to present my case! I keep a flip chart near my desk and a legal pad handy wherever I am. These are tools I use to communicate with people, and I make a point of always having them available. The advent of multimedia software and laptop computers provides an even more extensive arsenal of presentation tools.

If I didn't approach my work this way, I would have to work even harder and longer to achieve the same results. By planning my presentations and thinking through what I am going to say to people, I am working more efficiently and actually saving myself considerable time in the long run. Presentation skills enhance my work ethic by making me more productive, and they also give me an advantage over my competition. Because I employ this strategy and do not leave my presentations to chance, I believe I hit more home runs than most people, and you can too!

Positive attitude. My friend and mentor Zig Ziglar gives a great description of what a positive attitude will or will not do. Zig says a positive attitude won't let him *do anything,* but it *will* allow him to *do everything better* than he would do with a negative attitude. I agree with Zig completely. My having a positive attitude will not allow me to do things I am physically or mentally incapable of doing. I can't run a 100-meter dash in 10 seconds, no matter how positively I might think about it. It just won't happen. But in areas where I do have some ability, a positive attitude enhances that ability and allows me to use it more effectively.

However, I have known some very positive people who never seem to accomplish much. They spend a lot of time being positive and talking about what they are going to do in the future, but they never seem to be able to turn their ideas and dreams into reality. It may be that they don't know how to present their ideas effectively to others. Since we need other people to take positive action in our behalf if we want to be successful, having the most positive attitude in the world will accomplish little if we can't motivate and move other people to positive action.

> *"You learn to speak by speaking, to study by studying, to run by running, to work by working; and just so, you learn to love by loving. All those who think to learn in any other way deceive themselves."*
>
> —SAINT FRANCIS DE SALES

Self-discipline and persistence. Some people think I am *too* persistent! It is true that I doggedly pursue opportunities and believe that just because someone says "no" the first time doesn't mean he won't change his mind later. In all likelihood, we have all heard success stories that resulted from someone making just *one more* attempt after a series of failures. As a matter of fact, every successful inventor, salesperson, or executive has probably experienced success only after previous failures, simply because of his self-discipline and persistence. You may have even experienced this phenomenon in your own life.

Self-discipline and persistence are definitely vital ingredients for success; however, we all probably know some people who possess these qualities and yet are not successful. It could be that they consider "persistence" as badgering people and hounding them until they give in, to the point of being obnoxious. Nothing could be farther from the truth.

No matter how tenacious we may be, our success will eventually hinge on our abilities to effectively communicate and present our ideas to others.

The first impression we make when we meet people often conveys whether we are the kind of person they could like and trust.

BUILDING A MENTAL SAVINGS ACCOUNT

The importance of communication and presentation skills becomes especially evident when we realize that we are creating a mental savings account in others every time we have contact with them. With each interaction, we deposit a small piece of ourselves in their memory; and the deposit is either positive or negative, depending on the way we present ourselves. The first impression we make when we meet people often conveys whether we are the kind of person they could like and trust. At first meeting, they can only make broad judgments about our physical appearance, conversation ability, and body language; but they deposit these impressions into their memory and keep them available for future reference. They have begun to form their impression, and that impression will determine their willingness to continue the relationship.

As time goes by, each time they are in contact with us, they deposit more information into their memory, and the more information they have, the better they know us. The way we act and present ourselves provides the basis for most of their impression of us. We are literally making a presentation of sorts every time we have contact with someone!

> *"Relationships of trust depend on our willingness to look not only to our own interests, but also the interests of others."*
>
> —PETER
> FARQUHARSON

Let's consider some important factors that could affect the impressions we make on others:

Being truthful. Truthfulness is the most important quality in human communication, because it establishes credibility. People prefer to deal with honest people.

Maintaining eye contact. People are usually suspicious of anyone who won't look them in the eye. Sometimes people may have trouble making eye contact simply because they are nervous or because they lack confidence.

Listening well. We have all known people who never seem to hear what we are saying because they are always talking. Or they seem to constantly interrupt us in mid-sentence to tell us more about themselves or respond to whatever we say with a story that "tops" ours. We must train ourselves to be good listeners if we want to communicate well with others.

> "Never fail to know that if you are doing all the talking, you are boring somebody."
>
> —HELEN GURLEY BROWN

Using positive body language. Since people are both listening to us and watching us when we communicate, our body language is as important as what we are saying. We need to be aware of how we are using our hands, face, head, and feet, and avoid gestures that distract from what we are trying to say.

Being "real." Since everyone knows that no one is perfect, there is no advantage to pretending that we are. If we let people know we need help, most of the time they will do their best to accommodate us. If we try to convince them that we are perfect and need nothing, that's exactly what we will get!

Clarifying objectives. When we are seeking assistance from others, we must have a clear understanding in our own minds about the objectives of the conversation or presentation. What do we want them to do? What do they need to hear to cause them to say yes? It is important that we understand the whole message we are trying to send.

Relating to our listener. In order to really communicate, we must learn to develop empathy for the person to whom we are speaking. This requires that we mentally put ourselves in that individual's shoes and try to imagine what he is feeling and thinking, and what his concerns are.

Adjusting vocabulary. As a general rule, we do not need to impress others with our vocabulary. It *is* our responsibility to understand the vocabulary of those we are addressing and to adjust our vocabulary to basically the same level. We know what we are saying, and we need to make it easy on our listeners.

Truthfulness is the most important quality in human communication, because it establishes credibility.

A good strategy is to mirror their exact words. For example, if they want to "leverage" and we want to "maximize," we need to immediately get into the "leveraging" business. However, we have to be careful to explain any technical terms or acronyms with which our listeners may not be familiar. Many times, communication never really takes place because of vocabulary disconnects.

Using the right medium. Everyone has his own preferred medium for basic communication. Some people prefer face-to-face meetings, others like written material, and some prefer e-mail rather than a fax or a letter. It is best to find out how others prefer to communicate with us and use that method.

What kind of mental savings accounts have you been building in the minds of others? I suggest you ask people who know you very well to rate you in these areas. Discuss with them areas in which you are strong and areas that you think need improving. If your ego and self-esteem will allow it, have improvement discussions of this type periodically with someone you trust. If you adopt these skills and use them in your contacts with others, I can guarantee that the deposits you make in their mental savings accounts will be more positive.

I hope you now see communication and presentation skills in a new light. These tools actually have the power to produce distinctions in us that will invite the positive action in other people that we need to complement and support our own goals and objectives. I believe those who most effectively integrate strong presentation strategies into their planning processes are well on the way to having that "winning edge" and elevating their own personal achievement level.

VIPs

(VERY IMPORTANT POINTS)

🏳 The people who become most successful are those who are able to skillfully convince and persuade other people to take action on their behalf.

🏳 When everything else is equal, the ability to effectively present and communicate ideas is the greatest single factor in success.

🏳 Life is a series of presentations, and our success is dependent upon how we present ourselves on a daily basis.

🏳 The first impression we make when we meet people often conveys whether we are the kind of person they could like and trust.

10

PRACTICE PRODUCTION BEFORE PERFECTION

Achievement is about producing results, and you can't produce results until you start doing things. If you do nothing, that is exactly what you will get—*nothing!*

As I mentioned earlier, I have developed a concept in my belief window called Production Before Perfection (PBP). PBP is a system that guarantees action and consistent results. PBP is the best antidote for procrastination I have ever employed, and it never fails! I can honestly say that PBP has been the most significant tool I have used— it has helped me earn millions of dollars over my career, it has generated huge successes for major Fortune 100 clients, and it has created a reputation for me that attracts business opportunities of all kinds.

"Waiting is a trap. There will always be reasons to wait . . . The truth is, there are only two things in life, reasons and results, and reasons simply don't count."

—ROBERT ANTHONY

Before I tell you more about PBP, I need to warn you. When you begin to practice PBP on a regular basis, you will be doing things that conflict with the belief principles of 90 percent of the people on this planet—and you *will* face resistance. PBP is not a "natural" thing for people to do, and you will hear many objections about why you should "wait" to do something. Pay no attention. Just forge ahead. You will achieve the results you want while they are still waiting.

WHAT IS PRODUCTION BEFORE PERFECTION?

PBP is based on a simple premise: A person does not have to have *all* the answers before he or she can start working! Nothing prohibits achievement more than procrastination, and the idea that everything has to be just right or even perfect before one can begin is the foundational concept that supports procrastination. PBP flies in the face of waiting and demands action *now*. The main idea of PBP is this: Act first and get it perfect later, as you progress. The person who wants to quicken achievement has no room for procrastination and needs to be very careful when tempted with the word "wait."

PROCRASTINATION

Every time I see a person who doesn't get results, my guess is that procrastination is involved. However, most people don't think of themselves as procrastinators because they have many reasons for not doing things *today*. And their reasons usually sound quite plausible. Procrastinators are experts at justifying inaction and can convince even the most alert observers that the best strategy is to wait—for something.

In Chapter One we discussed our windows of belief. Unfortunately, procrastinators really believe that their reasons for not doing things are completely valid. This means that procrastination is the result of incorrect thinking and their belief that something is true that really isn't. Procrastinators think they are being prudent and cautious, which will help them do a better job when they finally get around to doing it. Please allow me to insert a brief disclaimer: I do *not* recommend PBP for those responsible for launching space shuttles, repairing or flying airplanes, surgeons, or other individuals whose jobs require the utmost in precision to preserve our health and safety. This concept is not an absolute that applies to every situation, but it is definitely applicable most of the time.

"Procrastination is the art of keeping up with yesterday."

—DON MARQUIS

I authored a book called *Finding 100 Extra Minutes a Day*, and I have both taught this concept to my consulting clients and spoken on the subject for over a decade. As I have done so, I have conducted my own research; and I have discovered that people basically have five common beliefs that form the foundation for procrastination.

FOUNDATIONS OF PROCRASTINATION

"I can do it tomorrow." This may be the most frequently used justification for procrastination. The reason it is so popular is because tomorrow sounds so close to today. Waiting until tomorrow just doesn't seem like that big of a deal. Waiting just one more day won't upset too many people, and there are surely many good reasons to justify the delay. The weather will probably be better tomorrow. Perhaps we will be more rested tomorrow and will do a better job. Besides, we have other things we need to do today that are more important. This list could go on forever. Waiting until tomorrow is a simple dodge to delay action. Personally, when I hear the word "wait," it grates on my nerves like fingernails on a blackboard. The problem is that frequently tomorrow is always yet one more day away. In my experience, it seems that every new day brings with it a new batch of opportunities and things to do. If we are bogged down in the completion of yesterday's tasks, we can take ourselves out of the running for today's prize.

> *"In a moment of decision, the best thing you can do is the right thing to do. The worst thing you can do is nothing."*
>
> —THEODORE ROOSEVELT

"I don't have everything I need, so I'll wait." This is a very popular statement to justify inaction and waiting. It is a notorious excuse often used by salespersons to avoid making telephone calls to prospects. "I can't call them until I have the new marketing

brochure." "I can't call them until the new product line is announced." "I can't call them until I find out about the new pricing policy." "I can't call them until the hole in the ozone layer closes." There are so many things for which we *could* wait that it is possible to never have to do anything again for our entire lives! I believe that some kind of action can always be taken, regardless of the list of the things we think we need. All we have to do is be honest about it and look for what *can* be done.

The principle is this: If you don't think you have everything you need, start anyway.

One example is how I write and market my books. I use what I call a system of "Parallel Progress." I make progress on things currently happening parallel to other events. For example, I don't wait until the books are completed to begin selling them. I don't wait until the books are finished before I start creating the artwork for the book jacket. I do the writing, selling, and graphic design all at the same time. I even work on multiple books simultaneously. These are parallel events. Are these elements always perfect? No. However, most of the time, they are closer to perfection than not, and the time, effort, and resources it takes to incorporate "perfectors"—little tweaks and modifications—is miniscule compared to the normal process of the months it would take if I did not use this concept. There is also an added side benefit. By starting everything early, I am able to actually see the books come to life and make most adjustments along the way. Then, when the manuscripts are actually completed, I have everything ready to go. This cuts several months off the time it takes most authors to bring a book to the marketplace.

The principle is this: If you don't think you have everything you need, start anyway. If you need to fix something later, you will have the time to do it then, and you will be much farther along in the project that you would have been if you had waited.

"I can't do it perfectly, so I'll wait." The person who has this attitude is in serious trouble regarding procrastination, because none of us will *ever* do anything perfectly.

This excuse is often stated another way: "I need to do more research until I find the perfect way." My personal opinion is that we frequently don't know how to do something until we actually start. Many times, when we start doing things, we discover that they are much easier to do than they appear.

"I don't have time right now." I recognize that some things require more time to complete than we think we may have at a particular moment. But where do we get the idea that we have to be able to finish something before we can work on it? Let me go back to my book-writing example to make my point.

In most cases, a book is a collection of chapters. Each chapter is a collection of ideas about a specific topic. Each idea may have many sub-points. When I begin a book project, how many books would I complete if I thought I had to finish the entire book in one continuous work session? Probably none. For that matter, how many chapters of a book would I complete if I thought I had to write a complete chapter in one work session? I can tell you that very few chapters would even be started if I believed that. Let's go one step further. How many ideas in a chapter would be completed if I thought I had to fully develop every point of an idea in a single work session?

Sometimes, if there is only a brief amount of time available, only a few sentences or a couple of paragraphs might be completed. But the sentences and the paragraphs add up and turn into a chapter, and eventually into a book. The point is that having only a short amount of time is not a valid reason for not doing anything. In thirty minutes of time we can do thirty minutes of work that we will not have to do later. The result is that we will complete projects quicker and will not fall victim to procrastination. If we more or less ignore our watches and do what we can when we can, the results will speak for themselves.

"Someone else can do it better—I'll wait." This excuse often represents a lack of confidence. It is one that people will make to themselves but not voice to others. It is rooted in the fear of failure. Some authors and psychologists say that all procrastination is rooted in the fear of success. I am not a psychologist, but I think it is more likely that people fear failure more than they fear success. People don't want to look bad, and they are hesitant to put themselves in a position in which they might fail. Procrastination is a tool that many people use because they falsely believe it will save them from failure. The truth is that procrastination will guarantee failure.

> *"Putting off an easy thing makes it hard, and putting off a hard one makes it impossible."*
>
> —GEORGE H. LORIMER

People who use this excuse make the decision not to do something that needs to be done or improve something that could be improved because they are not sure of their ability to do it. Or they may have a great idea and fail to take action because they believe someone else would do it better. In truth, many of us have experienced these situations and have failed to take action on things that were good opportunities for us. That is the problem with this particular excuse; we miss opportunities to achieve and grow.

When you see something that needs to be done, and you have the opportunity to do it, don't let someone else seize the opportunity. Be bold and step up to the task. If you are the first to see that something needs to be done, you are probably the best person to do it.

A BAD HABIT

Procrastination is probably many things, but it is mostly just a bad habit. Someone once said, "Repetition strengthens and confirms." Simply put, this means that the more we do something, the easier it gets! I believe we learn how to procrastinate over a long period of time, and the more we do it the easier it becomes. We practice this habit on a subconscious level, and it is not the result of a conscious, positive decision. It is more a reaction that seems to have a life of its own.

Habits, whether positive or negative, take time to form, and they are extremely difficult to break. Positive habits can become as natural as bad habits. If we are in the habit of saying "thank you," it is something we do naturally and spontaneously. If we are in the habit of exercising daily, it becomes a part of our routine. The longer we exercise, the easier it becomes. If we develop the habit of looking for opportunities rather than looking for failure, we will do it naturally. It will be a habit.

The best solutions are simple, and when we overthink problems we can make them more complicated than they need to be.

However, habits *can*, with practice and persistence, be broken! I am not saying it is easy to break the habit of procrastination, or, for that matter, any other habit. But I am saying it is possible, and the first step is to recognize that procrastination is, indeed, a habit—a habit stimulated by erroneous principles in our belief windows.

I am not an advocate of complicating things. I believe the best solutions are simple, and when we overthink problems we can make them more complicated than they need to be. In our culture today, many psychologists have taught us to look at problems in ways that are too complicated for most of us to understand. As a result, I see people wallowing in their problems over a long period of time. It is almost as if they are procrastinating about doing something about their own recovery by doing perpetual research.

I believe that habit problems are easy to identify and that solutions to those problems are simple. A person who is in the habit of doing something destructive has learned that behavior by repetition. Breaking a destructive habit involves simply practicing the *opposite* behavior long enough to allow that positive behavior to replace the destructive habit.

Sometimes people are very protective of their bad habits. Either they think the habits are somehow beneficial, or they have a fear of letting them go. They really believe they need them in order to remain happy and comfortable. Unfortunately, that is the way habits ultimately serve us over a long period of time. The procrastination habit is no different.

I believe procrastination can be eliminated if we will start forming different habits that stand in opposition to our procrastination habits. There are certain things we can start doing that will choke out procrastination, and if we will develop the habit of doing those things, procrastination doesn't have a chance. It is similar to getting rid of weeds in a one-acre lot. Simply pulling the individual weeds in a yard that size is not very effective. However, if the growth of the grass is stimulated, the root structure of the grass will eventually be so strong that the weeds will be choked out. The yard will be in the "habit" of growing grass rather than weeds.

In this analogy, let me point out that the key to success is focusing on the issue of the grass. If the focus is on getting rid of the weeds, that is where the lawn-tender will spend his or her time, money, and energy. If, however, the focus is on how to make the grass grow, that is where the efforts will be invested. It is the same with overcoming procrastination. We should not focus on how to stop procrastinating, but should focus, instead, on how to get more things accomplished. Getting things done will "squeeze out" the procrastination habit.

FORGET PERFECTION

Practicing PBP will help you develop habits that will choke out procrastination. Remember, PBP means that you start doing things immediately, regardless of what you think you need to make it perfect. It may mean that you will have to do some things twice or rework some details; however, it is well worth it, because you will get things done quicker. If you don't think you have all the information you need—start anyway! If you don't have all the tools you need—start anyway! If you do something that turns out to be wrong, use the mistakes to clarify the final vision. Start *now*. Get something moving. It is easier to get up to speed if you are already rolling.

Remember that success is the accomplishment of predetermined objectives, and action is the key to achievement. All of the things we have talked about have been geared toward helping you take action and achieve more. It begins with what you believe, and it culminates in what you do on a daily basis. Procrastination is the destructive habit that can wreak havoc with success, and it must be eliminated from your life if you want to quicken personal achievement.

VIPs
(VERY IMPORTANT POINTS)

- Nothing prohibits achievement more than procrastination, and the idea that everything has to be just right or even perfect before one can begin is the foundational concept that supports procrastination.

- If we are bogged down in the completion of yesterday's tasks, we can take ourselves out of the running for today's prize.

- Procrastination is a tool that many people use because they falsely believe it will save them from failure. The truth is that procrastination will guarantee failure.

- The best solutions are simple, and when we overthink problems, we can make them more complicated than they need to be.

- Parallel Progress allows you to accomplish more things faster, rather than simply completing each task separately with chronological steps.

11

THE PRODUCTIVE POWER OF LISTS

In my discussion of the habit of procrastination in the previous chapter, I said that simple solutions are needed to correct problems— bad habits, in particular. This chapter is about a subject that is very simple, yet incredibly powerful and universally underutilized.

At the risk of sounding simplistic or even foolish, let me say that there is absolutely nothing complicated about making a list; but list making is one of the most powerful tools I use, and you should use it too. If you can develop the habit of list making the way I describe it in this chapter, I guarantee that procrastination will have no room to grow or flourish in your life. And if you can crush procrastination, your achievement level will skyrocket!

List making, the way I practice it, is a way of life. By that, I mean that it is the most significant tool I use to keep my entire life together and functioning. I use it with my staff, my clients, and even my gardener. If I

If you can develop the habit of list making . . . procrastination will have no room to grow or flourish in your life.

were to stop making and using lists, my success and achievements would be significantly reduced.

My list-making system has been developed over a long period of time, as I have continually expanded the way I use it. Like most people, I started by making simple "to do" lists. I wrote down everything I needed to do on a daily basis, numbered each item, and used it as a way to keep up with my tasks. As my business and my family grew, my list-making activities grew to accommodate both.

For my lists, I prefer for the most part to use the ever-trusty legal pad. I use computers and PDAs, but for me, the yellow pad approach has an edge on the three distinct features of every effective list:

1. It is easy to review.

2. It is immediately accessible to capture notes, make updates, mark completed items, and add new items.

3. It refreshes my memory and reinforces my priorities, as I am forced to continually rewrite the items I still need to complete.

These features are important to any list system in order to achieve the top four benefits of list making that I will discuss later in the chapter. Those who are so inclined and have the technical ability could certainly build a system with these features in Microsoft Outlook™, Lotus Organizer®, a Palm Pilot™, or another such tool.

I keep a master list of everything that is going on in my life, and I update it completely every twenty-four to forty-eight hours. In between updates, I make notes right on the master list. Those who use an electronic list may want to mark up the printout or use Post-It™ notes to capture thoughts, ideas, changes, new tasks, and completions in between on-line updates.

When I update my master list, I have my current master list in front of me, along with any Post-It notes and index cards I have accumulated since the last update. I then completely recreate my master list from scratch. What I have discovered is that manually writing and rewriting my lists forces me to be aware of the things I have not yet completed. There is brainpower found in the action of physically rewriting my lists frequently. Some say this effort costs time, but I say it is a supercharger. It reveals procrastination spots and helps me focus.

My master list contains every action item in which I am involved, in both my personal life and my professional life. This master list links to the "My Life" file in which I keep my personal goals. Using a pen, I divide a single 8 ½ x 11-inch page into enough columns and blocks to list everything I need to do, as well as the key things for which my staff members are responsible. I have a place on the list for new ideas and a place for suggestions I receive from others. I talk to many people in my "connection database" frequently, and the ideas I get from them are often written on my master list in support of my continuous improvement effort. Ideas for any of the fifteen subjects that I study on a regular basis will go on the list as a reminder until I have fully incorporated each idea to the point that it is automatic in my thinking. I also include calls that need to be made, items I need to purchase, and my top priorities for the upcoming day.

How important is list making to me? I get up early every day, and list making is usually the first thing I do. This process will normally take just a few minutes, but occasionally I may spend as long as two hours updating and recreating my master list. I refer to this list fifteen to twenty times each day, so it is well worth investing the time to create the list. Considering that I do this every twenty-four to forty-eight hours, this is, admittedly, a time requirement; but I believe the benefits justify the effort. I probably spend close to 400 hours each year making my lists. That is the equivalent of ten forty-hour weeks! I take the use of time very, very seriously, and I very seldom waste time. I am well aware that time is our most precious asset. I even count minutes! That should tell you how important I believe list making is to my success.

> *"The secret to success is constancy to purpose."*
>
> —BENJAMIN DISRAELI

I believe there are four very valuable benefits to list making:

1. IT ELIMINATES PROCRASTINATION. This is, by far, the greatest benefit. I can honestly say that I rarely procrastinate (notice I did not say "never"). In fact, I do exactly the opposite, since I am always doing things early. I focus on completing things ahead of schedule, and remaking my lists manually allows me to do that.

It is a rare occasion, indeed, if anything ever slips through the cracks or gets lost, because I am a fanatic about working lists.

2. IT ALLOWS FREQUENT REASSESSING OF PRIORITIES. Recreating lists frequently forces us to confront items on our list that don't seem to be progressing the way we wanted them to. When I first put an item on a list, I often (at least mentally) assign it a priority and a completion date. This item may have several sub-items related to it. If I find myself or my staff getting behind the power curve on some of the subtasks, this tells me I need to elevate the priority of the entire project. In the same way, I can lower priorities for similar reasons. If I did not recreate my master lists frequently, I would not be aware of these subtle factors, and deadlines would probably not be met.

3. IT ALLOWS TIMELY REASSIGNMENT OF TASKS. Updating my lists from scratch regularly also forces me to evaluate the progress being made on each item. When it comes to items assigned to my staff, it helps me spot problem areas and bottlenecks much more quickly. By being aware of these issues on a daily basis, I am able to reassign tasks if necessary, or to bring more help to a project to assist a staff member who may be overloaded.

4. IT PROVIDES MENTAL FREEDOM. I believe each of us has a finite number of "Conscious Attention Units" (CAUs). These are similar to megabytes of RAM. Every single thing we do or think about requires a certain number of CAUs to process. Our lists are much like external quick-access hard drives in which to store items that

> *Recreating lists frequently forces us to confront items on our list that don't seem to be progressing the way we wanted them to.*

are not needed for the immediate tasks at hand. Therefore, by making lists, we regain more of our CAUs for getting things done. Creating our lists each day provides a great deal of mental freedom and eliminates worry. When we consciously work through everything going on in our lives through the process of updating our lists, we don't have to wonder what is going on. This translates into peace of mind, because we are freed from the burden of having to remember details. Everything is on the list, and we know what is happening with every item.

There are probably other benefits from manually updating our master lists frequently, but these four are the most important. I believe that each benefit is significant enough to justify the time involved, but I cannot overemphasize the value of the peace of mind I gain by doing it. I know everything I need to know about my activities at all times; and except for the time it takes to update the list, it is a fairly painless process.

> *"It's not enough to be busy. The question is: What are we busy about?"*
>
> —HENRY DAVID THOREAU

THE MASTER LIST

One reason I like to use legal pads is that they are available in almost any store, and I hardly ever have to worry about not being able to find a fresh pad if I wind up somewhere without one. The key to list making is keeping it simple, and there is nothing simpler than using a legal pad and a pen.

I have developed a list system whereby I can get every item on one piece of 8 ½ x 11-inch paper. Sometimes I have to write fairly small, but that is not a problem since I am the only one who has to read the lists, and I can read my own writing (most of the time). I draw off blocks on the legal pad and allot one block for every category of information. The size of the blocks changes as the number of items in each category changes. There is no fixed number of blocks, since I have a block for each area of interest with which I am dealing at the time. I may create a block for a special project, and when the project is complete, the block goes away. I create blocks as I need them, and I try to remain very flexible. I use them in a way that fits the way I think, and sometimes I think all over the page at the same time. The point is, we should each create a master list form that works for us.

OVERCOMING ROADBLOCKS TO ACHIEVEMENT

Pace Productivity Inc. is a Canadian training and research firm that conducts productivity research. Pace recently published a report listing the top things that people say get in the way of their being productive and effective. Hundreds of people were interviewed, and the top responses were:

1. DISTRACTIONS—getting sidetracked and daydreaming

2. POOR PLANNING—poor time management and organizational skills

3. LACK OF FOCUS—doing too many things at once and not prioritizing

4. PROCRASTINATION—putting things off until later

Do any of the items on this list sound familiar? Let's see how list making can solve all of these challenges.

DISTRACTIONS—GETTING SIDETRACKED AND DAYDREAMING. We get sidetracked when we don't have a clear, daily list of action steps to help us maintain our activity and stay focused. When we keep a master list of projects and "to do" items, we are never at a loss for finding something to do that is important. When we work off lists, our minds are always attentive to the things we need to do next. There is no time to become sidetracked.

POOR PLANNING—POOR TIME MANAGEMENT AND ORGANIZATIONAL SKILLS. The very act of manually writing a master list will increase our organizational skills and allow us to make better use of our time. When we maintain a master list of our action items, it forces us to plan and schedule how and when all of the action items will be accomplished (and also gives us the opportunity to check items off as we complete them).

LACK OF FOCUS—DOING TOO MANY THINGS AT ONCE AND NOT PRIORITIZING. When we keep a master list, we become focused and refocused every time we update our lists.

PROCRASTINATION—PUTTING THINGS OFF UNTIL LATER. Procrastination involves a reluctance to start things. When we compile lists of action items, the making of the list is the actual beginning of each step. Simply by putting an item on the list means we have started working on it. This makes it a simple matter to continue working on it until it is completed.

OTHER TYPES OF LISTS

Creating and maintaining a master list of action items is not the only way I use lists. I am occasionally paid to facilitate high-level meetings for my clients as they conduct brainstorming sessions when stakes are high. The end product of these sessions is always a list of some kind. It may be a list of goals. It may be a list of specific things to do, or it may be a list of assets and resources that can be used to solve a problem. Lists always bring generalized discussion to a completion point, and I never consider a meeting over until an appropriate list has been created. This type of list-making activity is a formal step in the meeting management process that George Lowe and I recommend in our book, *We've Got to Stop Meeting Like This.*

Whenever I am meeting with a staff member, a customer, a prospect, or a vendor, I almost always close the conversation by making a list of the items we discussed and writing down the points we established or the actions we agreed to take. This brings closure to the conversation, and everyone clearly understands what has transpired and what his or her responsibilities are after the meeting.

Obviously, there are as many ways to use list making as there are people with ideas. Other effective lists may include a "call list" of people one needs to call each day, a "project ideas list" that will trigger future action based on the kernels of a good concept, or even a list of places (restaurants, perhaps) where one could have a good business conversation in, say, Atlanta, Detroit, or Baltimore. The possibilities are endless, and the benefits are enormous. A little more peace of mind comes with each list maintained.

You can clearly see the importance I place on list making. This may be the most significant thing we do on a regular basis that drives our achievement.

🚩

VIPs
(VERY IMPORTANT POINTS)

🚩 If you can develop the habit of list making, procrastination will have no room to grow or flourish in your life.

🚩 Recreating lists frequently forces us to confront items that don't seem to be progressing the way we wanted them to.

🚩 By making lists, we regain more of our Conscious Attention Units for getting things done.

🚩 Lists help us overcome roadblocks to achievement, which include distractions, poor planning, lack of focus, and procrastination.

CONCLUSION
THE WINDS OF CHANGE

As I have written this book, I have searched my heart and mind for truths that have contributed to my own success. I have shared with you both things I have done right and things I have done wrong. The ideas I have presented have been tried, tested, and proven—many by the successful people I have studied and modeled, some by my own trial and error, and all by my own journey to success.

As you have read this book, hopefully you have become aware of the reasons why you do the things you do and have discovered some of the things you need to change in order to accelerate your success. Now it is time to make some decisions.

Your success can only be as stable as its foundation. The foundation is laid in your mind, because the way you think determines what you do. The actions you must take to execute a plan for success require a tremendous amount of mental focus and emotional energy. Understanding why you are doing what you are doing gives you the power to make the *choice* to change your actions. If you are willing to change, you will. It is that simple.

I hope you understand how vitally important it is to have the *right* principles in your belief window to guide your thoughts and actions, for your long-term success is dependant upon the strength of this underlying pillar. An intimate and continually growing relationship with the God who created you and who knows all of your strengths and weaknesses, all of your successes and failures, and all of your past and future, will prepare your belief window to receive only those principles that are based upon truth. Then, by internalizing all the success principles you have learned, whether from this book or other sources, you will have developed a solid repertoire of beliefs that will take you to new heights of success. With the right principles in place, your life-management skills will improve, and you will develop a winning attitude. Your foundation will be ready, and you can start to build.

In the building process, the blueprints must be carefully followed, or there will be flaws in the finished product. As I see it, the blueprints of success are comprised of action; effectiveness; and planning, goal setting, and speed. How well you integrate those strategies into your plan determines how quickly you attain success. Again, it comes down to a choice: Will you make the changes you need to make, or will you continue doing things the way you are currently doing them? Please believe me—working through the details and developing your strategies are well worth the time and effort they take!

No matter how great your foundation or your plan, you cannot build success if you don't use the right tools. I have shared the things that have worked well for me—tactics that I have developed from years of study and application. I *truly* believe that if you utilize these tools—realize that your success depends on the help you receive from other people; learn to effectively model and benchmark the distinctions of successful people; improve your presentation skills; practice the concept of "production before perfection"; and learn the productive power of lists—your achievement level will skyrocket!

So, now it's your turn. If you will put forth the effort to change the way you have done things and do the new things you now know to do, prayerfully and with godly wisdom, you will achieve the results you want. Whether you have struggled for years to achieve the success you desire, or you simply want to reach a new pinnacle, I believe you now have access to all the elements that can take you to the highest level of achievement—and quickly!

ABOUT THE AUTHOR

TONY JEARY, known as Mr. Presentation™, is a published author, success coach, and business strategist. Tony is the founder of High Performance Resources, an international presentation and strategic planning firm serving Fortune 100 corporations as well as small businesses. He travels the globe coaching many of the world's top business leaders, including presidents and CEOs of corporations such as Sam's Club, Wal-Mart, Ford Motor Company, Shell, Texaco, and New York Life.

Tony's business experience is extensive. He has owned and operated more than thirty different companies and served as consultant for more than 500 organizations in more than 35 countries over the past two decades. He has had the privilege of working with and is endorsed by such business professionals as Zig Ziglar, Brian Tracy, Jim Rohn, Mark Victor Hanson, and Ken Blanchard.

Tony has authored more than two dozen books on personal and business development, including *Speaking From the Top, Inspire Any Audience, Designing Your Own Life,* and *The Good Sense Guide To Happiness.* He is also a voracious reader who studies and reviews more than 100 business and personal development books each year.

Tony believes that success starts at home. Tony, his wife, and their two daughters live by a family mission that focuses on the ideals of sharing, supporting, and helping others. They currently reside in Texas.

Tony can be reached at www.MrPresentation.com or through his business manager at 877-2-INSPIRE or 817-430-9422.

For additional information on seminars, consulting services, scheduling speaking engagements, or to write Tony Jeary, please address you correspondence to:

High Performance Resources, Inc.
8105 Firestone Drive
Flower Mound, TX 75022

www.MrPresentation.com

1-58919-026-2

$29.00

PRESENT LIKE A PRO—AND GET RESULTS.

Good presenters hold the audience's attention.
Great presenters inspire the audience to act—and act now.
Here's how you can be that great presenter.

Tony Jeary, Mr. Presentation™, delivers all the tips, tricks, and techniques you need to polish not only your presentation skills but also your ability to positively inspire any audience. Step by step—from planning your presentation to closing it with action-getting appeal—Jeary explains the vital basics as well as the finer points of presentation excellence. Loaded with quick tips and proven wisdom from the pros, *Inspire Any Audience* delivers the confidence and professionalism needed to succeed in front of the audience—any audience.

Additional copies of this book and other titles by
RiverOak Publishing are available from your local bookstore.

If you have enjoyed this book, or if it has impacted your life,
we would like to hear from you. Please contact us at:

RiverOak Publishing

Department E

P.O. Box 700143

Tulsa, Oklahoma 74170-0143

Or by e-mail at: info@riveroakpublishing.com

Visit our website at:

www.riveroakpublishing.com